Lectionary Stories *for* Preaching *and* Teaching

Pentecost Season Edition, Cycle C

for the Revised Common Lectionary

A Compendium of Stories from
StoryShare
a Component of **SermonSuite.com**
from CSS Publishing Company

CSS Publishing Company, Inc.
Lima, Ohio

LECTIONARY STORIES FOR PREACHING AND TEACHING
PENTECOST SEASON EDITION, CYCLE C

FIRST EDITION
Copyright © 2013
by CSS Publishing Co., Inc.

Published by CSS Publishing Company, Inc., Lima, Ohio 45807. All rights reserved. No part of this publication may be reproduced in any manner whatsoever without the prior permission of the publisher, except in the case of brief quotations embodied in critical articles and reviews. Inquiries should be addressed to: CSS Publishing Company, Inc., Permissions Department, 5450 N. Dixie Highway, Lima, Ohio 45807.

For more information about CSS Publishing Company resources, visit our website at www.csspub.com, email us at csr@csspub.com or call (800) 241-4056.

ISBN-13: 978-0-7880-2728-4
ISBN-10: 0-7880-2728-X   PRINTED IN USA

Table of Contents

Introduction   7

Pentecost Sunday   9
Acts 2:1-21
I'd Like to Thank...

Holy Trinity Sunday   11
John 16:12-15
Guided on the Path

Proper 4 / Pentecost 2 / Ordinary Time 9   15
1 Kings 18:20-21 (22-29) 30-39
Give Me an S...

Proper 5 / Pentecost 3 / Ordinary Time 10   19
1 Kings 17:8-16
Oh God... Please Don't Make Me Go!

Proper 6 / Pentecost 4 / Ordinary Time 11   22
1 Kings 21:1-10 (11-14) 15-21a
The Mayor's Wife

Proper 7 / Pentecost 5 / Ordinary Time 12   26
1 Kings 19:1-18
7 - 7-7-77

Proper 8 / Pentecost 6 / Ordinary Time 13   30
Luke 9:51-62; Psalm 77:1-2, 11-20
Confidence in Crisis

Proper 9 / Pentecost 7 / Ordinary Time 14   32
2 Kings 5:1-14
Being Helped in Spite of Himself

Proper 10 / Pentecost 8 / Ordinary Time 15   35
Luke 10:25-37; Psalm 82
Where Have All the Good Samaritans Gone?

Proper 11 / Pentecost 9 / Ordinary Time 16   38
Luke 10:38-42
Housewarming Warning

Proper 12 / Pentecost 10 / Ordinary Time 17   42
Hosea 1:2-10
I Have Loved You...

Proper 13 / Pentecost 11 / Ordinary Time 18   48
Luke 12:13-21
Then What Will You Do?

Proper 14 / Pentecost 12 / Ordinary Time 19   50
Isaiah 1:1, 10-20
Is Anybody Listening?

Proper 15 / Pentecost 13 / Ordinary Time 20   53
Isaiah 5:1-7
Donnie's Plant

Proper 16 / Pentecost 14 / Ordinary Time 21   57
Jeremiah 1:4-10
God Searches for a Spokesperson

Proper 17 / Pentecost 15 / Ordinary Time 22   60
Jeremiah 2:4-13
Thirsty for Living Water

Proper 18 / Pentecost 16 / Ordinary Time 23   63
Philemon 1-21
Terminally Shy

Proper 19 / Pentecost 17 / Ordinary Time 24   68
1 Timothy 1:12-17
The Biggest Sinner

Proper 20 / Pentecost 18 / Ordinary Time 25   70
1 Timothy 2:1-7
Hero

Proper 21 / Pentecost 19 / Ordinary Time 26   72
Psalm 91:1-6, 14-16
Be Not Afraid

Proper 22 / Pentecost 20 / Ordinary Time 27   75
2 Timothy 1:1-14
Caught Not Taught

Proper 23 / Pentecost 21 / Ordinary Time 28   78
Luke 17:11-19
The Outsider

Proper 24 / Pentecost 22 / Ordinary Time 29   82
Psalm 119:97-104
Deontologize the Principle of Parsimony

Proper 25 / Pentecost 23 / Ordinary Time 30   85
2 Timothy 4:6-8, 16-18
Looking Ahead

Reformation Day   87
Jeremiah 31:31-34
A Change of Heart

All Saints Day   90
Daniel 7:1-3, 15-18
Crazy Dreams

Proper 26 / Pentecost 24 / Ordinary Time 31   93
2 Thessalonians 1:1-4, 11-12
Small but Mighty Faithful

Proper 27 / Pentecost 25 / Ordinary Time 32   96
Luke 20:27-38
The Wrong Lens

Proper 28 / Pentecost 26 / Ordinary Time 33   99
Luke 21:5-19; Isaiah 12
In That Day

Christ the King / Proper 29   101
Jeremiah 23:1-6
What's the Stick For?

Thanksgiving Day   103
John 6:25-35
Bread

About the Authors   107

Introduction

Since you are reading this, you probably preach on a regular basis. It is important to not only bring God's word to the members of your congregation but to help make the gospel of Christ engaging and thought-provoking.

Most people know that Jesus, the Master Storyteller, very often used stories and parables to make an important point to his listeners about God's kingdom. Following his example, we know that helping people to understand God's word through the telling of a story not only provides additional interest in a message, but also makes that same message easier to understand.

Over the years, CSS has published thousands of relevant, interesting, and inspiring anecdotes and stories to season a pastor's sermon. Not only has CSS produced numerous books to aid pastors in this important part of ministry but CSS also has a weekly online service called **StoryShare**, a component of **SermonSuite.com**, that was created to bring preachers the most timely and relevant illustrations possible. This edition of stories and anecdotes, gleaned from **StoryShare** for Cycle C, are written to dovetail with the readings from the Revised Common Lectionary and will serve you well as extended illustrations or in many cases, stand-alone sermons.

It is our hope that the stories in this book will not only assist you, the pastor, in your preaching but will also help you throughout your ministry.

The editors at CSS Publishing Company, Inc.

Pentecost Sunday
Acts 2:1-21
by C. David McKirachan

I'd Like to Thank...

I'm receiving an award tonight. That may seem like small change to most of you but other than my degrees, a bronze medal in the Mid-Atlantic Conference, and some thank you's, I've never received an award. I didn't really notice that bit of trivia until I realized I had to write an acceptance speech. I've written books, sermons, lectures, essays, poems, eulogies, research papers, treatises, and songs, but I've never written an acceptance speech. That's when it occurred to me, I'd never been given an award.

"I'd like to thank the judges and my wife and my mom..." Somehow the models that I'd gleaned from the few times I'd stumbled or been pulled into the Oscar show didn't seem to fill the bill. I was puzzled and nonplussed.

Now what the heck does all of this have to do with the second chapter of Acts? I've always thought Peter's speech after the shakin' and rattlin' has to be one of the most in-your-face, lack-of-tact, slam dunks I've ever seen or heard. Then again such slam dunks rarely win hearts or influence people. I didn't think his was a good model either.

This award is from the American Conference on Diversity. The rabbi and I are both getting it for our work in "... championing the cause of encouraging, facilitating, enhancing, and helping to create inclusive communities." There's no mention of eating, drinking, laughing, supporting, sharing family ties, or being human together. But we're getting the award anyway.

On Pentecost the diversity of the world stopped being an issue. The Spirit blew through it like tissue paper. So much for all the reservations and prejudices that had taken who knows how long to build. People didn't stop being different, it just became secondary.

Okay, maybe that was a good way to start. So I did. Here it is, you get it first.

"Three years ago, I got married. I learned that being different is good. I'm a slow learner. She's a good teacher.

"If communities of faith are to have any authenticity or integrity in this post-modern age, we must reach toward something more than a recitation of our version of history or sad litanies of dogma. We must remember that faith is an affirmation of something far beyond our understanding or our limitations. We represent the presence of something that can never be limited or boxed. These two communities of faith have had a close relationship for decades. They will never be the same. But because of their relationship and because of their difference, they learn. And because of our learning, and in the midst of it, we rejoice. And I know that our God does too. Thank you."

It's not Jack Nicholson, but it's got a flavor of Pentecost. Did you know that's a Jewish holiday too?

Holy Trinity Sunday
John 16:12-15
by Peter Andrew Smith

Guided on the Path

His grandmother was waiting for him as soon as the ordination service finished.

"John, you've come so far," she said with tears in her eyes. "I am so proud of you."

"Thanks, Gran." John shook his head. "I can't believe it's real."

"Oh, it is." She straightened his preaching stole. "I always knew that you were going to be a pastor."

"You did?"

"Certainly, I knew since you were a little boy and came to live with us."

"I wish you had said something to me," John said. "It might have made my journey here easier."

"But I did tell you on numerous occasions," she replied.

John tilted his head to one side. "I don't ever remember you saying to me that I would be a pastor."

"After the accident when you came to live with us, the first thing I told you was that God was going to help us get through the terrible loss of your parents."

"I remember that. I didn't know what it meant because I'd never really been to church before I came to live with you and Gramps." John smiled. "It's hard to believe that there was a time when I'd never been to church."

"Especially now," his grandmother said. "When you started preaching this morning it was like you had always been a preacher. That's what I saw that first year when you helped your sister come to grips with what happened."

"I didn't think I helped that much."

"Oh, you did. You were caring and supportive and you loved her as much as you could." His grandmother tapped his chest. "That's when I knew God wanted you as a pastor."

"If you knew why didn't you tell me?"

"When you were a little boy who didn't know anything about being in church?" his grandmother asked. "You wouldn't have understood what I meant."

"So you didn't actually tell me."

"No, I did. I took you to church so you could come to know God and see what a pastor did," she said. "Remember Pastor Stevens?"

"I sure do," John said. "I still remember his voice filling the church. He sure could preach."

"That he could. He was the one who encouraged you to get involved in the youth group, wasn't he?"

"Yes, he did. It was a hard year keeping that group together after he left and before Pastor LeDrew came."

"You wanted to quit more than once. Remember what I told you?"

"That good things take work and God's things take persistence," John replied. "I remembered those words through high school chemistry and when I went to join the church."

"We were so proud when you stood up front and gave your life to Christ."

"I was never so scared," John said, "to see all of those people looking at me and not wanting to disappoint them or you."

His grandmother laughed. "I thought you were going to fling the pages of the Bible loose you were shaking so badly."

"I had never spoken in front of a group before. I was terrified."

"And you got through it okay." His grandmother patted his hand. "The next time you read you weren't quite as nervous."

"I don't remember the second time I read in church."

"Christmas Eve when you couldn't find the reading from Luke and kept flipping through the Bible," she said. "You claimed after that you would never read in church again."

"I did?"

"Uh-huh. That was until Pastor LeDrew took you aside and told you the story about the time he announced a responsive psalm and then read a different one his first Sunday in a new church."

"I remember him telling me that." John laughed. "But I read in church a lot before I went to college."

"You certainly did because I wouldn't let you give up sharing that clear strong voice you have."

John narrowed his eyes. "That's how you told me I was going to be a pastor… by encouraging me to be a leader in the church."

"Telling a boy who was terrified to read in front of people that he was going to be a pastor would have been overwhelming. I pointed you in the direction I knew God was calling you and let you find the way," she said.

"The Holy Spirit was working through you."

"Me?" his grandmother said. "There was nothing holy or special about what I did. I just kept encouraging you. You're the one God is working through. You're the pastor."

"You really believe that God is working through me?" John asked.

"Of course I do and so does the church," she pointed at his robes. "You've been ordained."

"Then why don't you believe me?"

"Believe you?"

"Yes. Why don't you believe me when I say that the Holy Spirit was working in your life when you raised me?"

"But I didn't do anything special," his grandmother said.

"You took me in and helped me to know God. You guided me past my fears so I could answer my calling," John said. "I think that is special."

His grandmother waved her hand. "Lots of folks raise their children and grandchildren right."

"Does that make it any less special? I remember 'There are lots of people who follow Jesus but all of them are important in God's kingdom' being taught to me when I was a boy," John winked.

"John, you know it's not fair to use my own words to argue with me."

"They were good words for me to hear," John said. "Why aren't they good for you to hear?"

His grandmother paused. "Do you really think God used me to help make you a pastor?"

"Yes," John said. "I know it. The same as you knew I would grow up to be a pastor in the church."

His grandmother stood there and stared at him for a moment. John wrapped his arms around her. "God bless you for your faithfulness, Gran. God bless you."

Proper 4
Pentecost 2
Ordinary Time 9
1 Kings 18:20-21 (22-29) 30-39
by Keith Hewitt

Give Me an S...

The room smelled of pizza and desperation, with a hint of despair. A slice of cold pizza lay face down on the carpet, a casualty of an interception and touchdown — the same play that had caused the pizza pan to go sailing across the room, taking a nick out of the wall next to the TV and leaving behind a smudge of sauce. Marilyn scooted forward in her seat and perched at the edge while the figures on the screen lined up for a kickoff, her elbows resting on her knees, her face cradled in her hands. Her lips moved silently as she tried not to listen to the announcers' inanities.

"You have got to be kidding me!"

She jumped in her seat, head snapping up from her hands, immediately grateful that she had been to the bathroom during the official timeout. "What!?" she exclaimed, turning toward the voice. "Who the — How the —?"

The figure sitting on the couch gestured toward the TV without looking at her, said matter-of-factly, "They're down by twelve, with a minute and ten seconds left — pretty much the only way they can win is to run the kickoff back for a touchdown, recover an onside kick, and then drive down for another touchdown — all without any timeouts. Why not just part the Red Sea, while we're at it?" Eyes turned toward her, then, and the intruder's head shook slowly. "And you — seriously?"

"Seriously what? What did I do?" she demanded, forgetting the TV for a moment.

" 'O God, if you're really out there, give me a sign — let them pull this off,' " the figure — was it a man or a woman? — quoted, eyes turning upward piously at the end, before rotating back down to stare reprovingly at Marilyn. "Skipping past the 'if you're really out there' part, do you really think that's an appropriate use of prayer?"

"It's a playoff game!" Marilyn answered indignantly.

"Right. Playoff. There's an earthquake about to happen in China, North Korea is getting ready to light off another atomic bomb, and there's an airliner flying between Rio and Madrid with only one engine working — but this is a playoff. Of course you would want God's attention focused here."

"I thought God was — you know, everywhere. And all-powerful."

"Doesn't mean he can't be annoyed by all this piddlin' stuff. And for the most part he doesn't do things himself — he's kind of a big picture guy. He sends us to do them."

"So you're an —" she trailed off, hesitated.

"Yeah, that's me. An angel. And I can tell you, we don't like wasting our time." The visitor gestured toward the TV again, chided wearily, "Look, be reasonable. We don't get involved in this stuff anymore. You've gotta know people are praying for both teams. We don't pick sides — it's just not that important. It doesn't really affect your life — it shouldn't, anyway. If it does, you've got other problems."

"But I — wait, you said don't get involved in this stuff anymore?"

"That's right. If we did, Aaron Rodgers would have been MVP in 2010. But we had to let that slide."

"But you have gotten involved in it, in the past?"

The angel seemed to hesitate, then shrugged. "Well — let's just say there were some new procedures put in place after the 1967 NFL Championship. You know: Twenty below, Bart Starr, thirteen seconds left, on a quarterback sneak." The angel sighed. "Turns out, Dallas was supposed to win that game. The Old Man wasn't happy, so we had to make sure it wouldn't happen again."

There was a long pause, and then the angel went on. "And that brings me to the other reason for my visit. You said, 'O God, if you're really out there, give us a sign.' That's kind of insulting."

"How is that insulting? I'm expressing a rational question, a rational doubt —"

A raspberry from the visitor cut her off. "A sign? You want a sign?" the angel continued. "How about looking up at the sky or looking really closely at a flower? Entropy says things go from a more ordered state to a less ordered state — but, somehow, the universe went from chaos to a much higher ordered state. So take a deep breath or listen to your own heartbeat — you are an impossible marvel."

Marilyn frowned, looked puzzled, but didn't say anything.

"Look, you people, you're always asking for a sign — it's a constant game of what-have-you-done-for-me-lately. 'God, listen to me — if you don't do what I want you to, I won't believe in you.' You wonder why God has gray hair in all your paintings of him? It's because of you!" The angel waved a hand toward the outside world. "The rest of the universe is all neat and orderly — a wonder. But you people have to question it. You have to question him. It's like you're reading a book, but because you can't actually see the author standing in front of you, you're not really sure anybody wrote it."

Marilyn looked down. "I'm sorry. I didn't mean it that way."

"Maybe, maybe not, but that's how it came out. It's hurtful."

"I'm sorry," she repeated. "It's just — you know, this is important to me."

"God really does answer prayers, Marilyn, but the purpose isn't to prove himself to you. The purpose is to grant those who believe in him some small graces, from time to time — and also to show his power and glory to those who don't believe. You know, Daniel in the lion's den, Elijah versus the priests of Baal, that sort of thing."

She blinked. "What?"

"Never mind. You know, it wouldn't hurt you to sign up for a Bible study — I'm just saying. It would look good on the ol' permanent record."

Marilyn's eyebrows drew together. "What do you mean?"

"Never mind. The point is, God isn't Cris Angel or Lance Burton, performing wonders for your amusement. There has to be meaning, otherwise it's pointless. But I wanted to come by and let you know you were heard."

"Oh — well... thank you. I guess."

The angel nodded. "No problem. And now, if you'll excuse me, I have a few thousand more stops to make." As the figure of the angel faded, the head shook slowly. "I hate the playoffs," the angel muttered, the voice hanging in the air afterward.

Marilyn hesitated, straining to see as the image went away, finally shook her head and turned to the TV once more. Somehow, it didn't seem quite as important, now.

But she did wait for the clock to run out before she turned it off...

Just in case.

Proper 5
Pentecost 3
Ordinary Time 10
1 Kings 17:8-16
by Rick McCracken-Bennett

Oh God...
Please Don't Make Me Go!

John was reluctantly beginning to sense that his time at First Church was drawing to a close. Reluctantly, because he loved the church, he loved the people, he loved the work they did in the community in Christ's name — and because, he had to admit, he could do his work in his sleep.

And that was probably it... that he realized that he hadn't done anything new there, preached any new word, or led the church into a new vision of God's call to them in a very long time. He had told others facing the same situation that churches need different gifts at different parts of their life cycle. He really believed that but only when it applied to others. Certainly he had the gifts necessary for the next phase of life at First Church. Or if he didn't, he could learn them.

Still, it was bothering him enough that he took Bill, a lay leader in the congregation, to breakfast to tell him what was on his mind. "So you're thinking you might be called to go somewhere else — probably some bigger, better place in your mind," said Bill. "You know, I would believe in this 'calling' business a little more if just one of you took a 'call' that paid you less than the place you were leaving!"

Maybe it was Bill's criticism or maybe it was really the call of God — but John took a call to a little, dying church in a little, dying community. The pay cut was one thing, the loss of other benefits still another, but the biggest loss of all was the loss of prestige.

Being the pastor of First Church came with many perks — Rotary Club membership, a golf membership at the country club, a seat on the United Way board. Now the most he received was a clergy discount at the mom and pop restaurant in town. It was also quite a blow to go from preaching to 850 people to preaching to 45 or 50 on a good Sunday.

The village of his new little church was soul-sick and very tired. The closing of the wheel-bearing plant drove many out of town, and the drought that had lasted for several years now threatened to bankrupt just about everybody else.

Every night John would pray that God would reveal to him why he was sent to this God-forsaken place. Was he only here to officiate over the burial of the church and maybe even the town? Was he being tested? And even though he knew better, he asked God what he had done to offend God and deserve this.

The only thing he thought he heard back was "love them." That was it, just "love them."

The folks there were generous and asked him over to dinner just about every night of the week. Certainly they didn't have enough money to put on such a meal but each and every one was a meal fit for a king. And the collection — it was not what you would expect. Nothing like First Church, mind you, but generous. You might call it the "widow's mite." And John did love them and pleaded to God for them and asked them to sacrifice for those less fortunate.

Before his first year was out, the church had stocked a pantry for those in need, served breakfast each weekday for the elderly, and begun an after-school tutoring program. All John kept saying was, "We need to do the work God has given us to do. God will provide. God will take care of us." He said it even when he had a hard time believing it.

The funny thing is, John's new church didn't die. As they sacrificed so dearly so that others would not have to suffer as much, God richly blessed them.

On Rogation Day, John and thirty or so of his parishioners went around the village and their part of the county blessing the fields and praying for seasonable weather. Specifically, they were praying for rain. Farmers would get off their tractors and join in the prayers. They had to believe that their God would save them. If he didn't… well, if God didn't, the outcome would be worse than most could bear.

In June, after all the crops had been planted, the rain began; a slow, soaking, wonderful rain that lasted for several days and then returned every few days or so. People declared that it was a miracle. Perhaps it was. But the bigger miracle was that John's faith was strengthened each and every day as he remembered the great works God had done in the lives of those people.

Oh yes… the church grew, too. It never became huge in size but it became large enough for them to double their efforts to serve those in need with what they themselves had been given. The drought was truly over.

Proper 6
Pentecost 4
Ordinary Time 11
1 Kings 21:1-10 (11-14) 15-21a
by David O. Bales

The Mayor's Wife

I only contacted you because she's gone too far, to an extreme that can't be imagined; and she does it so stealthily. I need someone who'll take seriously what only a few of us know fully: the depths this woman has sunk to.

I need your oath. Swear that what I say is completely off the record. My information must be anonymous. Agreed?

Good question. I chose you because of some things you've reported in the paper and because you're new in town. No one who's lived here long keeps a neutral perspective when it comes to the mayor and Mrs. Moore. You'll have to believe me, and I'll have to trust you.

You going to take out paper and pencil?

Tape recorder? I don't know. I don't want my voice in this. I'm serious about not being identified. Yes, tape is more accurate. But give me your word that when you transcribe this you'll destroy the tape. Paranoid, you think. I can tell. Well, listen and decide.

Robert D. Moore Sr. was mayor for twenty years, and now Robert D. Jr. has reigned for another sixteen. The behavior of Robert Jr.'s wife, Diane Moore, must be exposed. I've been around since the beginning of Old Bob's reign. He started the political plums and pork. Graft: dishonest, impure graft. He got kickbacks and protection money from anyone who worked for or around the city. The chief of police was in his pocket, and most council members too. But, and this is the point, Old Bob distributed money in all directions. By being free with his favors and only keeping a fraction of his gains, he became more and more secure in office.

But Young Robert D. didn't begin that way. That family attribute had to be acquired through marriage instead of by DNA. Diane worked for Old Bob in his last two administrations, and he handpicked her for his son.

Don't you see? Old Bob as much as trained her to take over, since he wanted his son and not a daughter-in-law to be the next mayor.

You're new in town. All you know about Mrs. Moore is her charities. She follows the "small percentage" theory of her father-in-law. She takes a lot, distributes most in favors, and maintains her philanthropic façade, but even a small slice of her extortion and blackmail is a great deal. Last week your paper displayed her on the front page with another charity for disabled children. Her goal is to be pictured at least once a month in your paper. Most people know her that way.

No, never had children. Don't think they tried.

Technically, she's his secretary. But she directs the mayor. If he gives an order when she's not there, they wait and phone her to check what she wants. Few city workers don't owe her favors. Or she holds knowledge of an indiscretion over them like an anvil ready to drop if they don't tow the line.

Her photo in your paper kicked me over the edge. I was at that event. Had to be there — all shirt-and-tied up. I'd just come from the courthouse where she as much as celebrated her greatest victory. She did it her way, not with balloons and banners, but with a smirk. The mayor's door was open. I saw her smile in the mayor's office. I saw her newspaper smile and that did it.

Twelve years ago Terence Bailey was elected as district attorney. He was Young Bob's pick, and he won handily. He followed orders for the first two years. Then, even though he wasn't breaking open the organization, he started prosecuting cases he shouldn't. She warned him — politely, of course. He did it anyway. Not a huge rebellion. He argued that he must prosecute some flagrant crimes. If he didn't, the whole administration would rip apart from public outcry.

As far as Mrs. Moore was concerned that wasn't his call. I was walking out of the mayor's office when word came Bailey was making his first forbidden prosecution. Mrs. Moore said, "Oh he is, is he?" She smiled that left-handed little smile, and I knew she'd break him if it took half her fortune and the rest of her life.

Last week... What was that? Over there. Sounded like somebody. Didn't you hear something? Guess I'm jumpy.

Last week's newspaper with her picture included the story of Bailey's resignation. I've got my suspicions of how she did it. When your paper was delivered to his desk, Young Bob held it up so she'd see her picture on the front page. She said, "Give me that." She thumbed to the second page, dropped the paper onto his desk, pointed to "D.A. Resigns," smiled slightly, touched her finger to her temple, and walked into her office. She got him. Took her ten years.

Don't look so skeptical. No, I can't *prove* it. I'm telling you we're dealing here not with just an evil person but with intelligent wickedness. You can dig around a little. I think you'll find others who might say a few things — some older guys nearest to retirement, particularly in the city streets department. We took flak from the public when they caught us blacktopping the mayor's driveway.

Will you look into it? And I need your word that you'll transcribe this and not include my name. No matter if Young Bob loses the next election, Mrs. Moore is owed enough favors and knows enough secrets to rule this city until she dies. I have your word that you'll look into this?

*This document was discovered in a manila envelope behind a file cabinet when the **Herald** newspaper building was sold.*

Included was the following portion of a newspaper article:

WIDOW OF EX-MAYOR HONORED

Mrs. Diane Moore, 94, was laid to rest Saturday in the largest funeral since....

Proper 7
Pentecost 5
Ordinary Time 12
1 Kings 19:1-18
by Scott Dalgarno

7 - 7-7-77

It might be called a "slam dunk" today. The prophet Elijah faced down Ahab, the king of Israel; his spitfire of a wife, Jezebel; and along with them, 100 prophets of Baal. There on top of Mount Carmel he made fools of them all and showed once and for all who was God in Israel.

And then, wonder of wonders, what can only be called a great depression settled upon the prophet; a "darkness visible" to use the words of the novelist William Styron. Instead of exulting, the prophet slunk off to a cave like an African pachyderm waiting for his end.

The story of such a splendid hero reaching his lofty goal and then crashing shortly after is, yes, hard to understand but it also happens to be quite common. Here is an account of one such modern hero.

On the seventh day of the seventh month in 1977, at seven in the evening, Englishman Harold Abrahams dined for the last time with his compatriot Arthur Porritt. They had met for dinner at the hour of 7 p.m. on the seventh day of July every year since that lucky date in 1924 when Porritt and Abrahams knelt, nearly shoulder to shoulder, at the beginning of what Abrahams would later call "the loneliest ten seconds of my life."

That day, in Paris, the two managed to bring more honor to England than any two athletes in the island's glorious history. Abrahams won the gold medal in the 100-meter and Porritt took home the bronze. To the joy of every European in attendance, they ran the favored American champion, Charlie Paddock, off his feet. The race was greeted with such joy in England that (along with the success of their teammate Eric Liddell in the 400 meters) they managed to raise the status of track and field on Shakespeare's sceptered isle from a minor to a major sport. Would the Oxfordian Roger Bannister have broken the four-minute mile thirty years later without them? Probably not.

So what caused "the fastest man in the world" to go into such a steep mental decline in the wake of his greatest triumph? Perhaps it was the same thing that drove him so hard to excel. Running wasn't a passion for Harold Abrahams, it was a self-confessed compulsion. Harold Abrahams ran not because he loved to run but because he hated being Jewish.

More than anything else, he wanted his ethnicity not to matter in an age and country where it mattered way too much. It was as if he always had an asterisk after his name. Even when he met the Prince of Wales after his great victory he felt that he wasn't the gold medalist from England — he was the Semite medalist. In a word, for Harold Abrahams, running was a "weapon," a weapon he could wield against all the self-satisfied English he believed were his true opponents in life. It was anger at them and what he believed they thought of him that fueled him as he tore down that 4 foot x 100 meter strip of real estate that made his name in British athletic history.

It was also that anger that made him do something no British Olympic sprinter in history had ever done — hire a personal trainer. Sprinters had run forever on heart. Harold Abrahams was the first Englishman to run with his brains. In the 1920 Olympics, Abrahams had failed in the quarter-finals of both the 100 and 200 meters. He hadn't come even close. Four years later he was a different kind of runner. His first afternoon at the oval with Sam Mussabini had changed everything. Born in London of Arab, Turkish, French, and

Italian ancestry, Mussabini, like Abrahams, was *persona non grata* with his nation's athletic elite. That made the two all the more a team. They'd show the Cambridge snobs Abrahams went to school with what a champion looked like.

Mussabini was able to spot Abraham's troubles immediately. "You're overstriding," he said. Big strides were fine for distance but they meant death for the sprinter. That bit of wisdom, along with the advice that Abrahams should focus on the 100 meter race and a sensible training regimen were just what the Jewish sprinter needed. That and one more thing: a proper attitude as he peered down the lonely 100 meters.

By the time of the big Olympic day (7 p.m. on July 7, 1924), Abrahams admitted to butterflies — gargantuan butterflies. A self-confessed neurotic, he said that for four years he'd been so afraid of the thought of losing; now (he could hardly believe it) he found himself just as terrified at the prospect of winning. Mussabini had an answer for that too: "Only think of two things — the gun and the tape. When you hear the one, just run like hell until you break the other."

And he did. Harold Abrahams won. And after the initial exultation came the plummeting. He had worked so hard. He had dreamed of the moment for so very long. He had proved so much, and still, he had come up... empty. Was it simply a case of doing the right thing for the wrong reason? No one could say but Harold Abrahams — and he wasn't talking.

In time he got over it. Marriage to a good woman helped. So did breaking his leg in competition the next year. He had nothing left to prove anyway, and now he could devote himself to the law and a new side career — sports journalism. The British public adored hearing him on BBC, and they told him so.

Most importantly, once he'd proved himself on the track and made peace with a new life off of it, he began to hear a still small voice — a voice that told him it was time to make peace with his ethnicity. He had tried hating being Jewish — that hadn't worked. Why not try embracing it? He did and in time he became president of the Jewish Athletic Association.

At 7 p.m. in the evening on July 7, 1977 (7-7-77), Harold Abrahams and his friend Arthur Porritt dined together for the last time. They were old men now. They had known what it meant to fly high, and they knew what it meant to come back down to the ground. Abrahams knew what it meant to hit it hard, but he also knew how to bounce. Resilience was the key to happiness — that and not taking yourself too seriously. He would leave that to others. He was happy to die forgotten. Little did he know that in five years the world would take note of his Olympic triumph in the Academy Award-winning film *Chariots of Fire*.

Proper 8
Pentecost 6
Ordinary Time 13
Luke 9:51-62; Psalm 77:1-2, 11-20
by Argile Smith

Confidence in Crisis

Regina and Sam enjoyed watching movies together. They liked "cliffhangers" most of all, the kind that kept them sitting on the edges of their seats from the first flash of the story on the screen until the first frame of the credits. One day at work, they decided to take in one of the summer action thrillers that had just been released. The movie previews boasted a lineup of top-shelf superstars, and the take-your-breath-away storyline promised to be nail-biting, to say the least. They could hardly wait until the Saturday afternoon matinee.

On Friday afternoon, Sam overheard a conversation outside his office door. Two people at work were talking about the movie that he and Regina planned to see the next day. Although he didn't want to eavesdrop for fear that the information would ruin the fun for himself and Regina, he simply couldn't resist the temptation. He listened in and found out how the movie ended.

Not wanting to disappoint Regina, who had been looking forward to the chance to see the movie that had been getting such rave reviews, Sam kept what he had heard outside his office door to himself. On Saturday afternoon the two of them made their way to the cinema, bought their tickets, loaded up on popcorn and sodas, and sat in their favorite seats, ready to experience a movie buff's version of a rollercoaster ride.

Regina sat munching her popcorn and anticipating the thrill of what would happen next, thanks to all sorts of twists and turns in the unfolding story. Sitting next to her, Sam registered a little less anticipation. After all, he knew how the movie would end before it started.

The movie turned out to live up to the reviews. Regina hardly had time to settle into her seat before one shocking surprise after another jolted her. Like other good movies, the flick throttled her imagination into hyper-drive. At every twist or turn, her mind raced ahead of the story to figure out how it would end. By contrast, Sam sat there, enjoying the movie but not getting anxious about how the story would turn. He registered a quiet confidence that everything would work out just fine. As Regina whispered her hunches about how the story would end to Sam, he sat quietly and chuckled under his breath.

At one point in particular, there were hints that the lead character might be killed off in a chase scene involving nuclear-powered jet airplanes streaking across the sky like lightning bolts, weaving and in and out of mountain ranges with laser guns blazing. Sam didn't take the hint seriously, however, and for one good reason: he already knew that the hero wouldn't be killed. In fact, he even knew that the hero would win the day and give the movie a hand-clapping happy ending.

At the end of the movie, Sam confessed to Regina that he had kept what he overheard about the movie from her. His confession helped her to understand why he didn't get anxious as the story unfolded. His confidence had come from what he knew.

The Psalmist wrote about his quiet confidence in the Lord as he faced the twists and turns in his life. Likewise, Jesus reflected a deep sense of confidence as he faced the rejection of the Samaritans, the angry prejudices of the disciples, and the wafer-thin devotion of people who wanted to follow him. His confidence came from what he knew.

Proper 9
Pentecost 7
Ordinary Time 14
2 Kings 5:1-14
by Sandra Herrmann

Being Helped in Spite of Himself

> *Elisha sent a messenger to Naaman, saying, "Go, wash in the Jordan seven times, and your flesh shall be restored and you shall be clean." But Naaman became angry and went away, saying, "I thought that for me he would surely come out, and stand and call on the name of the Lord his God, and would wave his hand over the spot, and cure the leprosy! Are not Abana and Pharpar, the rivers of Damascus, better than all the waters of Israel? Could I not wash in them, and be clean?" He turned and went away in a rage.* — 2 Kings 5:10-12

"Jenny, call the travel agency, please. I need to leave on the first available flight to Norway. I'll need a hotel the first night but after that I'll be living on an oil rig. I won't need a car; the oil company's picking me up and delivering me."

"I'll get right on it, Mr. Daniels." Jenny called the agency and asked for her favorite agent. Sarah had taught Jenny the ins and outs of booking flights, and Jenny had taught Sarah what services her boss wanted. It was a perfect working relationship, one that Sarah had worked to establish. Unfortunately, Sarah was helping another customer at the moment.

"I can have her call you as soon as she's done," the receptionist told Jenny. No need to leave a number; Jenny and Sarah were in each other's rolodexes.

Jenny went back to working on the papers on her desk.

A few minutes later, Mr. Daniels strode out of his office, and stopped short. "What are you doing, Jenny? I need that reservation, and I need it right now!" He was red in the face and scowling. Even the papers in his hand were shaking.

"Mr. Daniels!" Jenny was shocked. Her boss had never treated her this way. Something must be wrong. But when she asked, he shook the papers in her direction and ordered her to "Make that call! Right now!"

"I already have, Mr. Daniels. Sarah, our usual agent, was helping another customer. She'll get back to me in just another minute or so."

"Why on earth would you need to have Sarah? Any agent can book a flight. Now get on it!"

Jenny looked down for a second, and then nodded. "I'm calling even as we speak."

Apparently satisfied, Mr. Daniels stomped back into his office. Jenny waited as long as she thought she could, listening for Mr. Daniels as she did so. An extra minute would possibly assure that she could get Sarah on the job.

Just as she had dialed, Mr. Daniels was back at her desk. "Well?" he demanded.

Jenny held up her index finger to show him she was waiting for the phone to be answered. When the connection was made, she asked the receptionist, "Is Sarah available yet? Oh, good. Yes, I can hold." She winked and nodded at Mr. Daniels, who was still standing at her desk.

"Hold? Jenny, this is possibly the most important trip I'm taking this year. And you're on HOLD? Why, may I ask? And it had better not be that you're holding for Sarah. Get hold of an agent and do it now!"

"Mr. Daniels," Jenny said in her best professional, calming voice, "I don't know why you're so angry. You only told me five minutes ago that you need this flight. It always takes about ten minutes to do a booking. And Sarah is the best person in that office. I trust her to do all of the travel plans that we need, and she's never let us down."

Mr. Daniels stopped pacing and shaking but he was still a bit red around the edges.

"You remember your last trip to Sweden? She was the one who found the artist your wife is so fond of and got you that wonderful print to take home."

Mr. Daniels was beginning to look sheepish. "Was she the one who did that? I thought you did that."

"Well, we both get credit for that one. I remembered the artist's name, and she knew which gallery carried his work. Trust me, Mr. Daniels. We want Sarah to book your trip and hotel. She always gets it right, even the extras."

"Well, all right," he said grudgingly, "Get her on the job as soon as possible." He was no longer stomping as he returned to his office.

Jenny was never so glad to hear anyone's voice as she was to hear Sarah's. "How can I help you today, Jenny?"

"Oh, Sarah, Mr. Daniels needs to get on the first available flight to the North Sea. Something's brewing on an oil rig up there, and he's really anxious. I've never seen him so uptight."

So Sarah made all the arrangements, including a cab to pick up his suitcase before picking him up and delivering him to the plane. "Oh, and Jenny, should I have a box of his favorite chocolates on the table in his room when he gets there?"

Jenny smiled. As she had told Mr. Daniels, Sarah always came through. Even with the "extras."

Proper 10
Pentecost 8
Ordinary Time 15
Luke 10:25-37; Psalm 82
by Rick McCracken-Bennett

Where Have All the Good Samaritans Gone?

Jesus said, "A man was going down from Jerusalem to Jericho, and fell into the hands of robbers..." — Luke 10:30

Save the weak and the orphan; defend the humble and needy; rescue the weak and the poor; deliver them from the power of the wicked. — Psalm 82:3-4

The way I figure it, sermons ought to be done by Friday morning. If I don't have it ready by noon on Friday I go into a slow but urgent panic.

This particular Friday, though, I didn't have a clue. The weekend was already packed and there wouldn't be a moment to work on it. Life got in the way of my preparation, and I knew I had some heavy lifting to do that morning or things might not go well that Sunday morning.

The office wouldn't work; the week had been filled with distractions that promised to continue. So I left home early with legal pads, lectionary helps, a jotted note or two, and I drove to my favorite coffee shop. It was never quiet but somehow I always seemed to get work done there.

As I approached I found myself behind a van going at about minus ten miles an hour. "This is just how my week's been going," I said, punctuating it with a palm hit to the steering wheel. As often happens though, this van had a reason — a good one. She was driving on about the worst flat I had ever seen; tire shredded and rolled under, the rim carving a groove in the pavement.

She made it... sort of, into the parking lot. Parked... sort of, and as I slid into a slot nearby the woman got out with her three kids in tow. It was probably the worst flat she had ever seen as well.

So... my dilemma was to help her and not get my sermon done or get my sermon done and feel (appropriately) guilty for days. Reluctantly I decided to help, and I prayed a quick prayer to God asking that I not be too embarrassed by my preaching effort on Sunday. Maybe this wouldn't take too long.

But of course, it did. As I found the jack and the spare that hadn't been off the van in ten or so years and blocked the wheels with bricks I had in my car (don't ask!), I began to get the story.

Careful to spare her daughters a description of the brutal truth they had all experienced, she told me a little of her story. She was recently divorced, and I got the idea that it was a nasty one. She had her daughters and little else. They were on their way across the state to her sister's, where they hoped they could get a new start and enough distance from the mess they were leaving behind to have some bit of hope in a better life. And then came the flat — the proverbial straw.

I began to resent the hundred or so cars that streamed through the drive-through line without so much as a query as to whether we needed help. I might have done the same thing before that morning, but not now; never again I promised myself.

Eventually I finished, put the ripped-up tire in its place, gave her directions, refused her offer of money, and went inside, where I washed my hands, wiped some of the tire crud off my shirt, ordered a coffee, and just sat there, not knowing what in the world I would preach about.

She and her daughters came out of the restroom and walked over to my table. "Girls," she said, "I want you to remember something about what happened here this morning. Do you remember the story of the good Samaritan? Remember? We read it just a few weeks ago." They all nodded. "Well, this man is our good Samaritan. While others went on by, ignoring our situation, he helped us."

I told her that the amazing thing was that the gospel for that coming Sunday was the story about the good Samaritan, and that I had come there to write my sermon. I thought for a moment and asked if I could tell this story. She said, of course. And the girls all thanked me. The little one gave me a hug, and I held back tears until they left and drove away.

I wasn't a real "good Samaritan," not even close. My feelings about this interruption to my day reminded me that I wasn't as "good" a person as I tried to appear. But that day, that morning, whatever I was — or became as God and this woman and her kids and I converged — felt good. And miracle of miracles, I had my sermon.

And I wonder… who was really the good Samaritan that morning and who was neighbor to whom? I think I know. And I know it wasn't me.

Proper 11
Pentecost 9
Ordinary Time 16
Luke 10:38-42
by David O. Bales

Housewarming Warning

"We need four of the medium-sized canopies. I don't know the exact dimensions, but I've seen them at other parties. Look at where I want them and you figure out the size. One here." Betty Jo pointed to the front yard and continued to walk to the side of the house. "One here." She rounded the corner to the backyard. "And two here: one on each side of the patio."

"I think I can handle that," Steve said. He started across the lawn to his pickup, parked in the driveway.

"And Steve," Betty Jo said as she followed him, "I phoned them a month ago and they said they had dozens, so make sure to reserve them in white. I've seen multicolored canopies and they look like a circus."

"Right," Steve said. He groaned as he stepped into his pickup. Through the open window he yelled across the lawn, "I thought we retired and moved away to cut down our workload!"

Betty Jo laughed and shooed him away.

Betty Jo sat at the kitchen table and sorted through photos from the florist. Which arrangement would look best in the living room? In the dining room? Low centerpieces for the tables outside under the canopies. The phone rang.

"Hi Karen," Betty Jo said. "How's my faithful ex-neighbor? Tickets arrived. Great, and I've got your reservations at the Shiloh Inn. Check in Friday and out on Monday. I got a note from the Lairds. They're coming too. Like old home week.

"Yeah. I thought about it, but I'll be exhausted after Saturday. And really, we haven't looked too much this last month, living in a motel and all. But at least by being here for six weeks we got to see the last three and a half weeks of construction. You'll love it. Lawn and landscaping came almost instantly this week. The fellow who rolled down the turf said it isn't a wonderful idea to have a housewarming party on it so soon but with careful watering all summer it'll take root no matter what.

"Sure. Get settled and the party over, we'll find a church and a Bible study or a prayer group. We don't have the time yet.

"You sound like Steve. I just haven't had time. If you want to worship here Sunday, look in the telephone book and find the church. Tell the group to keep praying for me.

"Okay, looking forward to seeing you too and getting all our, dare I say, *old* neighbors from the land of the Umpqua together with our new neighbors."

Betty Jo was teetering on a stool, putting up crepe paper when Steve arrived. "We've got five days till the party," he said. "Do we need streamers up all week?"

Betty Joe put the tape in his hand, pointed him to the ceiling, and went back to the stove. "Ice. I just remembered," she said. "How about if you ask Lorna and... and... I forgot her husband's name."

"Phil."

"Yes, Phil. Why don't you walk over to Lorna and Phil's and ask them to get 27 sacks of ice for us on Saturday morning. That'll give us three sacks at the end of each canopy."

"24."

"What?"

"Twenty-four sacks. Four canopies, times two ends, times three sacks is 24."

"Oh, you tell them what to do." She smiled and waved him out the door.

She stirred furiously, one pan after another, all four burners producing meatballs, freezer containers on the counter waiting to store them until Saturday. The phone rang. "This is like the neighborhood's prayer group arriving by telephone. Karen Gillis just phoned. They're coming. How about you guys? Wonderful! I'll make reservations along with Karen and Ed. Please, I want to.

"Karen asked me too. Not yet. We get this party over and, sure enough, we'll have time to find a church. Can't live without that. You and Kent can worship Sunday morning with Karen and Ed. Scope it out for us. Let us know what you think so we can drop in there on a Sunday real soon."

The front door shut. "Steve's here. Got to put him back to work. Talk with you later."

She dashed from the phone to the stove and quickly stirred one pot after the other. With the back of her wrist she pushed hair up her forehead. She turned to Steve and said, "I'm a little diz…"

* * *

Betty Jo felt as though she had wakened and gone back to sleep a dozen times. She looked to the ceiling and didn't see streamers up yet. No streamers. Wrong walls. White. Steve was sitting in a chair next to her, holding her hand. He was slumped and unshaven. She tried to talk but felt a mask over her mouth and nose. She managed to open her eyes wider. Steve was laughing. No, he was crying.

When she woke again Betty Jo's mind was clearer, although she felt she was struggling up from the bottom of a swimming pool to become fully awake. Steve was asleep in the chair to the left of her bed. She heard a "beep beep" and looked up to a television monitor with her vital signs making lines across it. She slept again.

On the evening that Steve said was her third in intensive care she was fully lucid. Steve pulled aside the oxygen mask. She whispered to him that the party was off. He laughed as he stroked her hair. She smiled through two streaks of tears.

The next night, Steve stepped toward the bed. "Karen's on the phone and she's calling from the prayer group."

Betty Jo fumbled until she got the oxygen mask up. She motioned to Steve that she didn't want to talk. She smiled weakly and said, "Tell them, 'Okay, I have the time now.' "

Proper 12
Pentecost 10
Ordinary Time 17
Hosea 1:2-10
by Craig Kelly

I Have Loved You...

He instinctively flinched as the spit stung his eye.
"I HATE YOU! I HATE YOU! I WANT YOU DEAD! DEAD, YOU HEAR ME? YOU CAN'T DO THIS TO ME!"

As he rubbed his spit-coated eye, he was suddenly knocked into the bare white wall, leaving him momentarily dazed. When the haze cleared, he snapped his head up, fully expecting to see a fist rushing toward his face. What he saw, however, jarred him just as much as that fist would have.

The force that had knocked him over was actually two men dressed completely in white rushing into the room to wrestle the spitter down onto the hospital bed, wrapping leather restraints around her wrists and ankles as she flailed about frantically, desperately trying to escape, perhaps to try to make good on her threat.

The sight of his wife tied down to a hospital bed stung worse than the spit. He turned away, his tears washing his eyes clean. He had known for a while that this had to be done, but knowing didn't make it any easier. He found himself leaning back against that white wall, using it to brace himself, fighting the urge to collapse into a heap of tears and despair on the cold, linoleum floor.

Behind him, he could still hear the cacophony of screams and expletives, with the clang of the restraints against the metal bed railing providing a chaotic rhythm. With the euphoria of her high now fully dispelled, the true music of her heart was now being played at full volume. No love, no joy, no peace, just chaos. Such was the woman he loved.

This drug rehab facility had promised "tough love," doing whatever it takes to break the spell that drugs had placed on their patients. However, seeing his wife in restraints screaming in agony, he didn't know if this tough love was aimed at the patient or the patient's loved ones. He looked back at her in her bed, knowing that if he could somehow take her place and free her from all of this, he would.

The screams eventually died down, replaced instead by quiet sobbing. She looked up at him, her eyes, now streaming with tears, filled with a pleading desperation instead of the red-hot rage that had been there not long before.

"Baby, please, please, let's just go home. I promise I'll be good. Things will be back to the way they were before. I'll be good to you, baby. I'll be so good. Just let me go home. I won't touch the stuff again, I swear." Her head fell back against the pillow, her tears soaking into the stark white pillow cover.

Just the way they were before? His mind went back through the years of their marriage. He knew she had a history when he married her. Yet all he could see was the goodness in her, the beauty. He loved her with an intense, white-hot, no-holds-barred love. It didn't make sense, but it wasn't supposed to. He chose her, not because of what she had done or even who she was, but just because he loved her. Did he need another reason?

And yet, practically from day one, her heart was not there with him. She *needed* — she *craved* — the drugs, the other men, the life away from him. He offered order; she wanted chaos. Even the child "they" had symbolized this faithlessness. He had no Asian in his ancestry, and yet his "son" had almond-shaped eyes. And still, he took that child in as his own. He knew the child wasn't his, yet he loved him with all the love he would give to his own son.

She would disappear for weeks, months at a time, hanging out with pimps and drug lords, catering to their every whim, desperate for another hit. He would drive through every dark alleyway and side street looking for her. At times, he would even see her leaning on a car, dressed in a tight, revealing top, short mini-skirt, fishnet stockings, and stiletto heels, selling herself to some nameless john. After a while, she would come home bruised, beaten, and half-naked, hoping he would take her in. And through the hurt and the rage — yes, *rage* — he felt, he still had that burning love for her. He would yell at her, scream, cajole, and even plead with her. Every time, after a while, he would find her gone, doing the same thing all over again. Every night he would cry himself to sleep, his arm reaching across the bed, longing to feel her body there, shuffling over to cuddle with him.

She wanted things to go back to the way they used to be? His blood began to boil. The white in the room began to turn deep crimson. *She wants to use me again? She wants to just keep me on a string, carrying me along while she does whatever she pleases? Does she not know the depths of my feelings, the passion of my love for her? Does she not know what I have continued to bring her out of, how I would keep taking her in time and time again? How can she keep doing this to me? NO! NOT THIS TIME!*

A guttural scream escaped his lips as he raised his hand to strike her. Her eyes grew wide and she began to tremble as she anticipated the pain of the blow across her face. His hand stayed up for what seemed like an eternity as she could see the rage that was once in her eyes now transferred to his.

His tears continued to stream down his deep red cheeks, practically ready to boil under the heat of his rage. Yet his hand started to lower. She started to smile, thinking his anger might pass once again.

Then he struck her.

When she was with the pimps and dealers, she had often been beaten. She had suffered broken limbs, rapes, deep lacerations, the works. More than once, she had been left for dead.

Yet this slap in the face hurt. It really *hurt*.

Without saying a word, he turned his back and walked out of the room. She looked up as she saw him walk out of the room and turn a corner. She wanted to scream after him, telling him to go to hell, but the words stuck in her throat. All she could do was lay her head back on her pillow and wail.

* * *

He looked somberly down at his desk. The legal papers were still there, sitting silently in front of him, waiting patiently. They had all the time in the world. At the top, printed in ink as black as midnight:

PETITION FOR DISSOLUTION OF MARRIAGE

His mind drifted back to the words he had heard hours (*Was it really hours?*) earlier: "As your attorney and as your friend, you've got to end this. Cut her off. Spare yourself this agony."

He looked up at the framed picture sitting on his desk. His wife was smiling broadly, the smile reaching, it seemed, from ear to ear. She was in her wedding dress, the white train flowing for what seemed like miles. Her hair was in a very becoming up-do, the brilliance of the red showing even through the veil. Her eyes sparkled like perfectly cut diamonds. She was radiant.

End it? Cut her off? Could he do it? Should he? He thought back to her wedding dress, the gleam in her eyes, her smile as she walked down the aisle. He remembered the love that pulsed through him like electricity that day. He thought back to the way his heart jumped every time he looked at her.

Slowly, he rose from his desk and walked over to one of the bookshelves that lined the walls of his study. He turned on the small bookshelf stereo and pressed the PLAY button on the CD player. The room was soon filled with the flowing strings and perfect choral harmonies of Bach's *Mass in B Minor*. He collapsed back in his chair, tilted his head back, and let the music flow through him.

He loved her. Even now, he loved her. All he wanted was to have her in his arms again, to wipe the past clean and start all over. He wanted to know that she would have the same heart for him that he had for her. He just wanted to love her.

But she hurt him. She cut him. She bruised him. He loved her, and she spurned him again, and again, and again. How much more of this could he really take? He knew that right now she couldn't be faithful if she tried.

But he loved her.

After a short while, the choir began to sing the *Agnus Dei*:

Agnus Dei, qui tollis peccata mundi,
miserere nobis.
Agnus Dei, qui tollis peccata mundi,
miserere nobis.
Agnus Dei, qui tollis peccata mundi,
dona nobis pacem.

Lamb of God, who takes away the sins of the world, have mercy upon us.
Lamb of God, who takes away the sins of the world, have mercy upon us.
Lamb of God, who takes away the sins of the world, grant us peace.

Have mercy upon us. Give us your peace. Take us back. Take me back. Forgive me.

His tears fell on the divorce papers, making the ink start to run. All he could do was sit there and cry.

Take me back. Forgive me.

Slowly he rose, wiping his face. Taking the tear-stained papers, he walked over to the corner of the room. The paper shredder let out a high-pitched whirring sound as he fed the papers through it.

He looked up, not smiling, but feeling a lightness and peace he hadn't felt in what seemed like years.

The day is coming. There will be reconciliation. I will take her back.

He walked back to his desk and raised the picture of his wife to his lips, kissing it tenderly.

"I'll see you again soon," he whispered as Bach's music filled the room.

Proper 13
Pentecost 11
Ordinary Time 18
Luke 12:13-21
by Argile Smith

Then What Will You Do?

Evan finally finished law school. The road to graduation for him had been paved with lots of ups and downs. Although his grades didn't show much promise, his lackluster academic record didn't pose as big a problem for him as his ego. His arrogance seemed to be his biggest flaw and it only got worse with each semester. Actually, Evan didn't register much concern about the way he barely passed his courses and warnings about his lack of potential for success didn't get much traction in his mind either. His dad had built a successful law firm in his hometown. Evan boasted more than once that his dad had an office for him once he graduated from law school. The certainty of the job waiting for him made him arrogant and careless.

Dr. McKenzie had watched Evan's bloated ego disfigure his perception of his future. He had enrolled in some of her classes, and she had tried to teach him but found herself getting frustrated with him. Evan's mammoth ego obstructed a clear picture of his foolish behavior.

Because Dr. McKenzie was a Christian, she noticed with concern an even more troublesome habit that plagued Evan. His arrogance about his place in his father's law firm had prevented him from factoring eternity into his life equation. She had heard him pontificate in class on the need to embrace life's adventures here and now with no thought of tomorrow. After all, he kept on insisting, we have the greatest fun when we live in the moment. He ignored serious consideration of his future.

On graduation day, Dr. McKenzie made her way to Evan at the reception so she could talk with him one more time before he left for good. She struck up a conversation with him by asking, "Well, Evan, now that you have finished law school, what's next?"

Evan replied with characteristic bravado, "Don't you remember? I'm going back home!"

"Then what will you do?" she asked him.

"Well," he said, seeing that he had an interested audience, "my dad's already got an office just waiting for me at his law firm. For as long as I can remember, he's told me that one day I would work with him. So now I am going to make his dream come true."

"Then what will you do?"

"My plan is to get my license, settle in my office, and work with my dad on a few cases to get a feel for it."

"Then what will you do?"

"I really haven't given it much thought. I've kicked around the idea of settling down, maybe getting married, buying a house. Things like that."

"Then what will you do"

"Oh, you know, have kids, take over the firm when Dad retires, maybe buy a boat."

"Then what will you do?"

"Doc, I can't really say that I've thought that far in advance. Maybe I'll give the firm to one of my kids and retire myself when I've got all I want."

Sensing that she was about to reach the end of Evan's patience, she asked, "Well, then what will you do?"

With her question, Evan let his frustration show with his reply. "I suppose I'll die like everybody else!"

Then she asked, "Then what will you do?"

In the parable of the rich farmer, Jesus showed the foolishness of failing to factor in eternity when we think about our future. So did Dr. McKenzie's conversation with Evan.

Proper 14
Pentecost 12
Ordinary Time 19
Isaiah 1:1, 10-20
by C. David McKirachan

Is Anybody Listening?

I volunteered as a guide for canoe trips down the Delaware River. That statement in itself is a story. It's enough to say that I was pastor of an inner-city parish at the time. I needed this like a sail needs wind. Johnsonburg Camp, in the wilderness of New Jersey (stop laughing), is a place of forests and holy connections. It drew me. I ended up on the board of trustees, but that's another story as well.

The canoe trips started at the camp with training and group-building, then we went by truck north into New York state to put in. Twelve senior high students and two counselors, 95 miles in five days — everything we used, including food, tents, sleeping bags, and frisbees, went into seven canoes. Canoeing is not what we were there to do. We were building and opening and expanding people — senior high students and decrepit old dudes as well. But with its demands and its joys and its thrills, the trip was a fitting context for growth. You learn a lot fast while negotiating whitewater or cooking meals when you'd rather lay down in the dirt and sleep.

There were always one or two who saw themselves as better than anybody else and set out to prove it. They were used to being large and in charge, or smart and capable, or all of the above. But a good amount of negotiating a river is counterintuitive. It's not something you can bully your way through, no matter how that has worked in other contexts. Experience is a great teacher. Listening to those who have an intimate knowledge of the river also works. Sometimes people prefer pain and humiliation to humility.

Two such lessons have to do with paddling faster than the current to allow steerage, and moving the back end of the canoe to let the current lever you off of rocks you may encounter. Both acknowledge that your strength is not as great as the river's. Both demonstrate that the water can be an ally, if you let it. And both demonstrate that what has always worked for you in other contexts may get you in trouble. "We always did it that way before" are very dangerous words.

Two characters inhabited what we called the NASCAR canoe, running ahead and proving that they were cool and powerful at every opportunity. They had inside jokes that they threw at the "pokes" and the "slugs." They were not allowed to get out of sight of the rest of us, but they flirted with this distance. Halfway through the morning they got to a nice set of rapids. They decided to demonstrate that the caution we exercised wasn't necessary if you were as cool as they were. In the middle of the whitewater was a good-sized rock dividing the flow. They decided in their testosterone-polluted minds to get there, climb out, and give commentary on our sad lack of skill as we went by.

By the time I realized what they were doing, they were backpaddling and slowing down — and then they landed broadside against the rock. NASCAR started filling with water. Rather than pushing the rear end around, they tried pushing off of the rock against the current. I went to the shore and jumped into the water above them. I could hear the aluminum screaming as it bent and the rivets popping like demonic corn. They climbed up on the rock and watched as the river wrapped the canoe around the obstruction like a shawl. Their equipment and packs and food took off downriver.

There was no need to chastise them. They'd been humiliated quickly and effectively. Whatever edge they thought they had on the group was gone and now they were in need. How far they had fallen.

We found most of their stuff along the way. But that night they slept on a tarp, while their sleeping bags hung in a tree drying. We had another canoe by the end of the next day. They'd been passengers for a while. Their racing days were over. By the end of the trip they began to laugh at themselves, a sure sign of health.

If only they'd listened. But maybe they needed the lesson. It's a terrible way to learn, but you know how pride is. It takes us places we never should have gone, invites us to do things others warn us about, and helps us to conveniently forget all the good advice wiser folk have offered. It reassures us that if we go through the motions of being nice people, we'll be fine. It leads nations to war. It invites us to forget about the poor, to forget about the ones who live in the margins, in the shadows. Isaiah knew. He understood the power of the river… and he understood the cost of forgetting.

Proper 15
Pentecost 13
Ordinary Time 20
Isaiah 5:1-7
by Stan Purdum

Donnie's Plant

My beloved had a vineyard on a very fertile hill. He dug it and cleared it of stones, and planted it with choice vines; he built a watchtower in the midst of it, and hewed out a wine vat in it; he expected it to yield grapes, but it yielded wild grapes.
— Isaiah 5:1-2

Although Lester was ninety years old, his health was still good and he was still able to take care of himself. He missed Sarah, of course, with whom he'd spent nearly 68 years, but he'd seen no reason to give up their apartment after she passed away the previous summer.

The only thing was, Sarah had been the outgoing one. She'd been the one who visited with their neighbors, chatted with the mail carrier, and made small talk with the children in the building. Lester wasn't unfriendly and he'd always said hello when he passed others in the complex, but he'd left the real socializing to Sarah. But now, with Sarah gone, Lester missed the human connection.

And so it was that he began to make an effort to be more talkative — and to his surprise, it wasn't as hard as he expected it to be. He became better acquainted with the folks on his floor and especially with the father and daughter who lived next door.

The father, a man in his thirties, was named Don, and his daughter, age nine, was Donnie. It had not always been just the two of them, but two years previously, Donnie's mother had been killed in an auto accident. So now the sad-eyed man and his bright-faced little girl were alone. Lester was never quite sure how much to say to Don, but Donnie made talking to her easy; she simply started conversations with Lester every time she saw him, and Lester made it a point to stop and speak back to her on each occasion. So eventually, the old man and the little girl began to think of themselves as friends.

Thus, it was not altogether surprising when one day in early summer Donnie came to Lester's door with a request. She was leaving the next day for a ten-day vacation with her daddy. Would Lester be willing to tend her plant while she was away? With little thought and without seeing the vegetation in question, Lester immediately agreed.

At daybreak the following morning, Don and Donnie started on their trip. Later in the morning, Lester stepped outside his door and found a child's small sand pail filled with nondescript dirt. Growing from this soil, but not thriving, was a fragile tree-like seedling. Competing with it for survival — and clearly winning — was a long reedy plant of some sort.

At that moment, Lester was struck by the enormity — and perhaps the foolhardiness — of what he had promised. A city dweller all his life, he'd never had a garden, and neither had he ever nurtured potted flora. But he *had* promised, and so, as he picked up the bucket, he uttered a prayer that Donnie's plant would not die on his watch.

A short time later, Lester told another neighbor about his dilemma and showed him the sand-pail planter. This man quickly identified the smaller plant as a maple tree seedling and the reedy stem as an obnoxious weed. This neighbor then invited Lester into his apartment and showed him his two dwarfed trees growing in pots. Learning of the special soil and nutrients this man used for his plants, Lester decided a trip to the local nursery was in order.

It was Saturday, and the large nursery Lester found was crowded and busy. After searching in vain for several minutes for a nursery worker to help him, Lester noticed a woman pushing a dolly loaded with shrubs. When he approached her, however, she indicated that she was a customer herself. But as Lester turned to walk away, he heard an inner voice say, "Turn back; this woman will help you."

So Lester obeyed. He changed direction and this time he told the woman he thought God had directed him to her for help. Who knows what the woman thought about that, but she politely stopped and gave him her attention. Lester introduced himself and told his story, and when he was done the woman, who introduced herself as Debbie, said that yes, she would help him. She left her dolly where it was and led Lester with his cart to various stops around the store until he had everything he needed to give the tiny tree a fighting chance — potting soil, fertilizer, plant food, and a larger pot. She then went back to her own shopping.

Lester slowly made his way to the checkout line, and when he arrived, he found himself in line behind Debbie. As they chatted casually, it must have become clear to her that Lester was still feeling out of his depth. She told Lester that she operated a small flower business herself. And then she said that if he would bring his supplies and the sand pail over to her shop that afternoon, she would handle the transplanting for him. With great relief, Lester said he would.

When Lester got to Debbie's shop that afternoon, Debbie immediately took charge, expertly separating the seedling from the weed and bedding it firmly in good soil in Lester's new roomy pot. Then, picking up the other plant, she said, "This is only a weed; we'll just throw it away."

"We can't do that," Lester said. "Donnie thinks that is part of the plant."

Debbie thought for a second and then said, "I know what. We'll replant it in the pail." She dumped out the original dirt, filled the little bucket with potting soil, and placed the weed in its new home. Before Lester left, she gave him specific instructions on how to care for both of his botanical charges.

For the remaining time Don and Donnie were away, Lester followed Debbie's instructions to the letter.

Thus, when dad and daughter came home, the little girl was thrilled to find her tiny maple tree flourishing, and the weed looking robust as well.

The next day, Lester heard a knock at his door. When he opened it, he found Donnie standing there beaming. In her hand was the sand pail containing the weed. "Thank you for taking care of my plant, Lester," she said. Then with both hands she extended the pail with its thriving weed and said, "This is for you."

As Lester accepted her offering, he told Donnie that he couldn't think of a nicer gift, and he thanked her for being so generous.

After she left, Lester realized that what he had told the little girl wasn't just a matter of politeness — he *couldn't* think of a nicer gift.

Proper 16
Pentecost 14
Ordinary Time 21
Jeremiah 1:4-10
by Rick McCracken-Bennett

God Searches for a Spokesperson

> *[The Lord said,] "Before I formed you in the womb I knew you, and before you were born I consecrated you; I appointed you a prophet to the nations." Then I said, "Ah, Lord God! Truly I do not know how to speak, for I am only a boy." But the Lord said to me, "Do not say, 'I am only a boy'; for you shall go to all to whom I send you, and you shall speak whatever I command you..."* — Jeremiah 1:5-7

So God says to this guy, "I need your help. The people aren't listening to me — again! I need someone who will speak for me and show them where they've gone astray. I need someone to call them back to me. It doesn't pay much, but you'd really be helping me out. What do you say?"

But the man says, "I wouldn't know what to say."

"Not a problem," says God. "I'll give you words. I'm just about done with the script now."

But the man says, "Oh God, I'd love to help, but I am an old man. I think I'll pass."

And God lets out a big, long sigh and goes in search of someone who can speak the truth to his people.

So God says to this middle-aged man, "I need your help. The people aren't listening to me — again! I need someone who will speak for me and show them where they've gone astray. I need someone to call them back to me. It doesn't pay much, but you'd really be helping me out. What do you say?"

But the middle-aged man says, "I wouldn't have any idea what I would say."

And God says, "Not a problem. I'll give you words to say. I'm finishing up the script as we speak."

But the man says, "Oh, I'd love to help, I really would. But I've got a job and a wife and kids. I'm afraid I'm going to have to pass."

So God lets out another big, long sigh and continues his search for someone to speak the truth to his people.

God comes upon a young man, fresh out of college. "I need your help. The people aren't listening to me — again! I need someone who will speak for me and show them where they've gone astray. I need someone to call them back to me. It doesn't pay much, but you'd really be helping me out. What do you say?"

And the young man says, "I took painting as my fine arts credit instead of public speaking. I wouldn't know what to say or how to say it."

And God says, "It really won't be a problem. I'm working on the script and you'll get a copy of it in plenty of time. All you'll have to do is read it."

But the man says, "I'd love to help, seeing that I'm young and an idealist and want to change the world, but I've got to get a real job so that I can pay off my student loans first. I'll have to pass."

God sighs a little longer and louder now, and continues his search for someone — anyone — who will speak the truth to his people.

So God says to this teenager, "I need your help. The people aren't listening to me — again! I need someone who will speak for me and show them where they've gone astray. I need someone to call them back to me. It doesn't pay much, but you'd really be helping me out. What do you say?"

And the teenager pulls his iPod earbuds out of his ears and says, "Huh?"

"I said, I need your help speaking to all the people of the world since they stopped listening to me."

And the teen says, "Like... well, you know, I like wouldn't know what to say, man."

And God says, "Not a problem. I'll give you all the words you need to say. I'll even read the script into a podcast, and you can listen to it and just tell them what I want them to hear."

And the teen says, "Dude, I would like to help, but man, like I've got to hang out with my friends and stuff. Be cool... I'll pass."

So God tries one more time. He comes upon a young boy, hardly twelve years old, and says to this child, "I need your help. The people aren't listening to me — again! I need someone who will speak for me and show them where they've gone astray. I need someone to call them back to me. It doesn't pay much, but you'd really be helping me out. What do you say?"

And the child says, "But I'm just a kid. I wouldn't know what to say."

And God says, "Look, I'll write it down. I'll give you the words. Don't worry."

And the child says, "Sure... okay!"

Which just goes to remind us to never ask a man to do a child's job.

Proper 17
Pentecost 15
Ordinary Time 22
Jeremiah 2:4-13
by Peter Andrew Smith

Thirsty for Living Water

"That's our church." Jim pointed at a large white building with a tall steeple along the street they were walking.

"Wow, that must be a beautiful place to worship," Sam said as they continued past stores and offices. "Who is your pastor?"

"Um. Tall fellow. Pretty good speaker. I think his name is DeSoya or DeSalle something like that." Jim paused in front of the church to squint at the sign. "Oh Desilvo. That's right, that's his name."

Sam chuckled as they resumed their walk. "I guess you don't get to Sunday service very often."

"We went regularly when the kids were in Sunday school. When Mary got sick I was there every week." Jim shrugged. "Since then I guess we got busy. You know with the girls moving out on their own we like to take advantage of the weekends."

"How long has it been since Mary finished chemo?"

"Seven years last March," Jim said. "That was a scary time let me tell you."

Sam patted him on the shoulder. "But you got through it."

"We did." Jim rubbed his eyes. "It was amazing how many people helped. It seemed like everyone I met on the street asked about her and told me they were praying for us. Good people in this town, you know."

Sam smiled. "Sure seems like a great place to live and raise a family."

"The absolute best place," Jim said. "It has been a great place to retire too — you saw the golf course."

They walked in silence for a few moments enjoying the sights of the small town.

"So why are you so unhappy?" Sam asked.

"What do you mean? Life couldn't be better for Mary and me. We've got time, good pensions, and we're both in good health. We're on top of the world."

Sam stopped and looked him up and down. "So why are you so unsettled?"

"Why do you mean?"

"Since Patty and I arrived, I've watched you do everything and nothing. You're up and down and down and up and can't stay still. You were always on the go but now you seem uncomfortable in your own skin."

"Huh." Jim shifted his weight from side to side. "I guess retirement isn't what I expected."

"How so?"

"Something's missing and I can't figure it out. I should be content and satisfied. I've got everything I always worked for but it isn't enough."

"Things okay with Mary?"

"Couldn't be better. Retirement lets us spent time together like before the girls were born."

"The girls doing okay?"

"Better than we imagined. Sally is happily married and expecting her first child and Suzy is setting the world on fire with her job. They both are happy and we couldn't be prouder."

"So what's wrong?"

"I don't know." Jim scratched his head. "Everything is good. Mary's good. The girls are good."

"You miss work?"

Jim laughed. "Not in the least. I love being able to do what I want with my days. We've taken some trips and I've been spending some time painting. But I can't shake the feeling that something is missing in my life."

Sam turned to look back at the way they had come. "Do you think it might be God?"

"What do you mean? I still believe in God."

"I never said you didn't. But how long has it been since you went to church, read your Bible, or prayed? When did you last make time for God in your life?"

Jim blew out his breath. "I guess it's been a while."

"You used to tell me how important it was for you and how you didn't feel the week was right unless you went to church on Sunday."

"Yeah, I always felt something, a peace and certainty, when I went to church." Jim paused and rubbed his chin. "Well, what I felt is hard to put into words and explain."

"Is it hard to explain in the same way as what you feel is missing in your life now?"

Jim nodded and they walked in silence for a few more minutes.

"You and Patty staying until Monday?" Jim asked.

"That's the plan."

"What are you doing Sunday morning?"

"Why?" Sam said. "You have a suggestion about what we could do?"

Jim smiled. "I think I would like to go to church."

Proper 18
Pentecost 16
Ordinary Time 23
Philemon 1-21
by Scott Dalgarno

Terminally Shy

The irony of the thing, of course, was how much Ben's mother always hoped he'd find a nice girl. Right up to the day he turned fifty she continued to tell him about "that nice Anderson girl who works at the bank."

"She's hardly a girl, Mother," he'd say. "She's worked at the downtown branch since I was in college." Ben's mother just didn't know what to make of her son. She'd tell her bridge-playing friends he was just "terminally shy." It took a real terminal diagnosis for things to really break for him, romantically speaking.

Well, it wasn't the cancer that did it. He'd met Suzanne a couple of months before the results from the MRI came back. She was new in Providence and began attending the Quaker meeting as a way of getting to know some people. Funny, a woman choosing a group that sometimes sits in a room for an entire hour saying nothing at all as a vehicle for finding community. If Ben was terminally shy, Suzanne's timidity was awaiting a serious prognosis.

Up until she met Ben, Suzanne told friends she was a cat person. That's all she'd say when a friend would ask if she wanted to meet a certain single friend or cousin. Suzanne had no problems with stray kittens (she often had two or three around her apartment), but she said she had no interest in making a project of someone's alcoholic brother.

Ben never was that specific about relationships. He'd just say in a general way, "Women are like elephants to me.

I like to look at them, but I'd never want to own one." His childhood friends thought him funny — funny ha-ha... and just plain, you know, funny. They'd long given up trying to interest him in a blind date.

What was truly funny, looking back, was that they met not within the walls of the church they both attended but in a pew in civil court. Alice, a mutual Quaker friend, was divorcing her husband of ten years, and she had enlisted both Suzanne and Ben to testify that she was a good mother and not the wicked witch her soon-to-be ex was trying to paint her as. Blessedly, neither was asked to take the stand, but the proceedings lasted an entire day and the two found themselves sharing a tuna sandwich alone in the funky cafeteria the county had been running for a hundred years. Ben had forgotten his wallet and Suzanne insisted the sandwich was much too big for her to eat alone.

There they sat in silence, elbows on formica, until Ben said it sounded an awful lot like church. Suzanne nearly choked and following that respectful silence it seemed neither shut up for a moment until the tumor on his brain took Ben's ability to speak away for good.

"For good" — where in the world did that term ever come from? The only good in it was that Ben, who was so wonderful at making faces anyway, used every muscle in his body to tell Suzanne how much he loved her once he couldn't say those words anymore.

The oddness of the fact that neither could say they'd ever had a boyfriend or girlfriend for their first five decades of life was balanced by the rapid progress of their courtship — a good word for love that began in a courthouse. The day Ben got his diagnosis, Suzanne brought him home. The cats already loved him — especially his massive chest and soft stomach. It was Linda, Ben's mother, who was troubled.

Here, all she seemed to crave, even in her widowhood, was a suitable companion for her son — and now that he'd found one she felt wretched about it every hour of every day. "What was he thinking?" she wondered. "What kind of hussy is this woman who's kidnapped my only son?" Linda was beside herself. And who heard all about it twelve times a day? Ben's sister Karen, of course.

Karen did what she'd done all her life — just look her mom in the eye and nod. That was her job; that was always her default position on everything when it came to family. Her mother had always been very good to her and the unspoken bargain was that Karen would just go along with whatever her mother had in mind. Now all she heard over and over was "How in the world could your brother do this to me, to us, to this family?"

And all the time Karen was just so happy that Ben had found anyone at all. Here he had brain cancer and yet she'd never seen him so happy in her life. There was a quietness about him now, a serenity that no member of her family had ever exhibited before. The Reasoners (oddly named) were never known for placid calmness. It was like Ben had become a wise teacher or something, and it was like it had happened overnight — or at least it seemed like that. There was just something about the combination of a life-threatening illness and a first love that put him in this holy zone... and Karen's mother couldn't see it. It was like she thought Ben had just been taken hostage by the Scientologists.

One day at the dollar store Karen finally had enough of her mother running down her brother. He'd been hospitalized that week, and Linda had not shown any interest in going to see her son.

"Mother," said Karen, adopting a tone Linda had never before heard on Karen's lips, "Ben is happy. Doesn't that mean anything to you?"

Stunned, Ben's mother began to repeat what a betrayal this relationship was to the whole family.

"Mother," said Karen, "let me finish."

"But you asked me a question," said Linda.

Karen continued right on. "Mother, after 48 years it's my turn to talk." Linda quieted right down.

"Mother, when John and I divorced last year you were a brick. You stood by me as closely as any daughter could hope for. My friends all commented on it. They thought you were amazing, the way you supported me but never interfered. Angie said over and over she wished she had a mother like you. All my friends just thought you were a breath of fresh air when it came to a family crisis."

Linda opened her mouth to speak.

"Don't you dare say a word," said Karen. "It's taken everything in me to get this far with you."

Linda hushed up.

"Oh, Mother, I'm sorry, but with Ben so sick and so in love, and Suzanne such a tender support — Mother, I just don't even recognize you anymore. You won't even go see him. Mother, you haven't even spoken to him in a week."

"How do you know th…"

"Because he told me. It was like the last thing he was able to say."

Linda began to weep silently.

"Ben's hurt, Mom. He doesn't know how long he's got, and he can't bear that this short time is being eaten up by this bitterness in your heart. I don't know if you're jealous or just afraid of the scandal this might cause with your friends. Frankly, I don't care. All I care about is Ben — and Mother, don't you think it's a good thing that after all these decades he's finally, you know, a little bit happy?"

Karen took a breath there in the aisle by the cards, where they were looking for something for her mom's sister Ada, who was about to turn eighty.

"Mom, Ben wishes he could have met Suzanne thirty years ago. He's sorry. I know he's sorry the relationship isn't more, you know, conventional. But he doesn't know what he could say to you if he could speak. You have to be the one to open the door. And don't think we have all the time in the world. All I know is, well, the oncologist says that with this kind of tumor..."

Linda shuddered.

"With this kind of tumor, anything can happen at any time." That was all Karen could say. They went out to the car and headed home.

Halfway to Karen's, Linda said, "Take me to the hospital." Karen obliged her mother. They drove in silence. Under the entrance, Linda asked if she could go in alone.

"Of course, Mother," said Karen. Linda walked slowly, breathing a bit hard, all the way to Oncology. Though she had not been there, she knew the room number — 413.

The door was open, but only halfway. It took everything in her to open it wide enough to enter. The lights were dim and a curtain was drawn around the bed. Linda paused. She heard nothing — no sound at all.

The silence terrified her. It made her fear the worst. Summoning all the courage she could, she looked around the curtain. There she saw her Ben, asleep in the recliner, wearing his hospital issue blues. Suzanne was there too, asleep in the hospital bed. The bed and recliner were pushed together. There they lay, holding hands.

It struck Linda that she had never seen a more beautiful couple in her entire life.

Proper 19
Pentecost 17
Ordinary Time 24
1 Timothy 1:12-17
by John Sumwalt

The Biggest Sinner

> *The saying is sure and worthy of full acceptance, that Christ Jesus came into the world to save sinners — of whom I am the foremost.* — 1 Timothy 1:15

A handsome, clean-cut young man sat in the visiting room of the county jail one day looking out through the bars, waiting for his appointment with the volunteer chaplain from one of the area churches. He was dressed in an orange jumpsuit; his hair looked like he had just gotten out of bed, which he had, if you can call a thin mattress on a cement slab a bed. When the deputies arrested him three days earlier, in the hallway outside of the classroom where he taught science at the local high school, he had been wearing a blue dress shirt, a brown paisley tie that matched his penny loafers, and tan slacks. His hair had been neatly combed and there had still been a hint of the Old Spice aftershave that he had splashed on his face just before leaving for school.

He sat there thinking about the fourteen-year-old freshman boy he had befriended, and what everyone would think when the story hit the newspapers. Sexual molestation charges against a teacher were always big news. He knew he would never teach again and that going to the state penitentiary for twenty or thirty years was a good possibility. There was a knot in the pit of his stomach that had not left from the moment the handcuffs were clapped on his wrists.

Pastor Jack Pearson, tall, thin, a little past middle age, with patches of gray in his beard that matched his wrinkled gray pastor's suit, made his way slowly up the steps to the county correctional facility. It just happened that he was on call, filling in for another pastor whose husband had been in an auto accident. As he stepped off the elevator he caught a glimpse of the young prisoner's profile across the lobby through the visiting room window. Suddenly he was filled with a deep, almost debilitating dread. He didn't know this young man, but he reminded him of someone he had pushed out of his memory for years and years.

It had only happened once and he had never done it again, but the reality that he had once molested a young boy came rushing into his consciousness. No wonder he had not wanted to come when he got the call. No one had ever found out about what he had done, but he had always lived with the fear that one day that boy, who would now be about the same age as the young prisoner in the orange jumpsuit, would come forward and identify him. The pastor was hit with the startling realization that this could and should have been him and that he had deserved the same fate and until now had somehow escaped even his own self-condemnation.

What would he say to this mirror image of his younger, darker self? What right did he have to pray and offer comfort and hope in the name of Christ when he carried the same stain on his soul? He whispered a prayer, "Oh God, help me," as he slowly opened the door to the visitation room. And before he introduced himself or offered his hand, he sat down at the table, looked straight into the young man's eyes, and said, "I have been where you are now, and I don't know what to say to you except that I believe in the mercy that Jesus offers to each one of us. I have experienced some of his grace, though I certainly never deserved it, and I know that if Jesus can forgive me and love me after what I did, he can and will forgive you too." Then he reached out and took the young man's hand and the two of them wept together.

Proper 20
Pentecost 18
Ordinary Time 25
1 Timothy 2:1-7
by C. David McKirachan

Hero

His name is John. His last name settles the issue of ancestry. It has double o's and is pronounced like there's only one. No question, Dutch. He's a chaplain in Seabrook Village, a full-service condo city near us. He also attends our ministers' lectionary study every Thursday.

Big and lanky, full of strength and self-deprecating humor, he's a nice guy to have around. He was an Army chaplain. After he'd been with us a while we started to hear stories about Vietnam. Like most combat veterans, his stories are terse, leaving out horrors, leaving out blow-by-blows. None of that would make any sense to those of us who have never faced enemies whose express purpose in life was to take ours.

He told us one story about sleeping in the building or tent where they did chapel. He'd put his cot up against boxes of Bibles. Just like everything in the Army, they come by the pallet load when they come. So he built room dividers out of them and had a little privacy in the midst of one of the most unprivate environments imaginable.

The mortar attack came when he was sleeping. Shells were lobbed into the camp over all the barbed wire and claymores and machine guns that defended the perimeter so carefully. No specific target or agenda, only to disrupt and frighten and if lucky to maim or kill someone who was close to the explosion. Shrapnel, bits and pieces of superheated metal, made sure the kill radius went a lot further than the explosive concussion. This particular shell landed close, he didn't say how close, but close enough to send fragments tearing toward him, sleeping. He never would have known. After the attack was over and clean up commenced, he found furrows torn in the crates of Bibles, pages ripped. The Word of God had defended him. He kept one of the Bibles, torn and mutilated. He showed it to us. He told us, chuckling, that it made a great illustration. In my book, he's a hero.

But this isn't about Vietnam. This is about a bumper sticker he has on his compact car. It's not the kind of sticker you'd expect from a combat veteran who'd seen the worst an enemy could do. He told us he likes to go the PX at the local Army base and park his car in the row with all the others, most of which proclaim with their bumpers, "God Bless America." Bunting and flags and patriotic decoration continue the push. His sticker has no stars or stripes. It says very simply, "God Bless Everybody, No Exceptions."

Like I said, this guy's a hero.

Proper 21
Pentecost 19
Ordinary Time 26
Psalm 91:1-6, 14-16
by Rick McCracken-Bennett

Be Not Afraid

"You shall not be afraid of any terror by night, nor of the arrow that flies by day; Of the plague that stalks in the darkness, nor of the sickness that lays waste at mid-day."
(translation from *The Book of Common Prayer*, 1979)

I'm not sure where I first heard it, but I was told that the #1 most requested song by our military men and women at worship services in Iraq is the Bob Dufford composition, "Be Not Afraid." That didn't surprise me. With words like, *be not afraid* and lyrics that speak of *crossing deserts* and *passing through raging waters* and *walking amid burning flames* and *standing before the powers of hell* it's difficult to think of a song that would speak more directly to the danger our men and women face every day in their service to our country. Every time I hear the song, I get a vivid picture in my mind of a dusty tent chapel in the desert and our military singing the soothing words of promise.

It's a favorite of mine as well. During particularly tough days I'll make my way into church, pick up my guitar, and play it from memory. I find myself singing the song to myself as I drive to a hospital emergency room to comfort a family that has had the unthinkable happen to them. I sing it to myself whenever I forget, as I too often do, that God is with me, God goes on ahead of me, and that my God will give me rest. While I haven't had to worry too much about arrows that fly by day or plagues that stalk me in the darkness or sickness that lays waste at midday, we all see enough scary things in a single day to keep a horror novelist supplied with plot lines for life.

As I write this, these headlines are streaming into my computer from the internet:

> University Student Faces Terrorist Charges
> *Be not afraid*
> Lawmakers' plane evades ground fire in Iraq
> *Be not afraid*
> Four Ohio stores evacuated in bomb scare
> *Be not afraid*
> Warming could worsen inland storms
> *Be not afraid*
> Family buries second son killed in war
> *Be not afraid*
> Stoning death boys found guilty
> *Be not afraid*

There were more, and unfortunately, in the weeks since I wrote these words, hundreds of headlines just as frightening have been printed in the paper and read on the evening news. More than ever we need to hear the words of the song *be not afraid* and the even stronger words of the psalm, *you* shall not *be afraid.*

I'm not surprised that when I "googled" the words *be not afraid*, I got thousands of hits that included poems, songs, articles, books, and blogs, most of them reminding us to not be afraid for we have a God that is with us, goes ahead of us, protects us, and guides us.

Years ago, I began to practice a discipline that I learned from a book by Eugene Peterson. Peterson reminds us of the words of the young man in the tomb in Mark 16 that go something like this: "Don't be alarmed; you are looking for Jesus of Nazareth… he has been raised… he is not here… go and tell his disciples and Peter that he is going ahead of you to Galilee, there you will see him as he promised."

The discipline he suggests is that we paraphrase those words as we make our way toward what might be a difficult or dangerous situation. It might go something like this: "Do not be afraid. Christ is risen and has gone before me to room 736 at Community Hospital where he will meet me as he promised." My role then, after praying these words, is to pay attention when I arrive at my destination to what the risen Christ has been doing before I finally arrived. I find myself far less anxious about what I am to say or do and simply try to fall into step with the work that Christ is already doing in that place.

Then… for at least a while, I am able to not be afraid; of the terrors (or the terrorists) of the night, the arrows of the daytime, or the plagues that stalk in the darkness.

Proper 22
Pentecost 20
Ordinary Time 27
2 Timothy 1:1-14
by John Smylie

Caught Not Taught

I love the reference to Timothy's family. One can imagine Timothy sitting in his one-room home watching his grandmother pray. Perhaps as a child he heard the prayers not only of his grandmother but also of his mother as they prayed for him, for members of their community, for folks in their family and for the world. If Timothy was like every other little boy when he was growing up, out playing with his friends and then coming home after doing a few chores and perhaps making a bit of income for the family, one can imagine that coming home for him was like coming into holy space. His home was filled with an invitation to the almighty God to be present.

Perhaps for Timothy, faith was caught not taught. I suspect, as a young child, he did spend some time in study with his elders but I suspect even more their faith, the faith of his grandmother and mother was an ever-present and shining example to him. Something in them attracted him, and one can only imagine that he wanted to have the light that he saw present in them in his own life.

When I first became interested in healing ministry, I heard about a healing mission coming to our home church. It was at a time in my life when I didn't spend a lot of time at church but I did believe that God was a God who was powerful. Sometimes churches to me did not seem like places where God was present but rather little communities that were caught up with the bitter struggles, petty infighting, and very often filled with mean-spirited people. Later I would learn that churches are hospitals for sinners, not museums for saints — so I suppose it was good that those folks with all their struggles allowed themselves to be under the influence of the good news of Jesus Christ.

In any case, I was excited by the neighborhood church offering a healing mission to the community. I decided I would go. The man who led the experience, the healing mission, was the international warden of the Healing Order of St. Luke the Physician. His name was John Park. I guess if I was to look at that language now — the warden — I might wonder if it was a prison ministry. In fact it was a ministry that sought to set people free from physical, emotional, mental, and spiritual ailments.

John looked like my image of a kung fu master. He had a bald head and a chiseled face. His spirit was soft and gentle and yet when he laid his hands upon anyone the power coming through them was strong and tangible. The strength of Christ within him contrasted against his own deeply humble spirit, and I found myself wanting to be like him. This was clearly an example of faith being caught not taught. Here in front of me was a man who believed in the power of God, and allowed himself to be a channel of the same. How blessed we are when we have examples in our life — people — who reflect to us the height and depth and breadth of God. How blessed we are when the sound teaching of our Lord is not only spoken but demonstrated by a life that is dedicated and possessed by the passion of Christ and the presence of the Holy Spirit.

How blessed we are when there are those around us who radiate the love of Christ — John Park was one of those teachers for me and I find myself still desiring to catch a hold of the goodness and power of the Lord that was so present within him. Sometimes we may not be aware of the gifts we have — particularly the gift of presence — the

Lord's presence within us. Pray that we will be faithful grandmothers and grandfathers, mothers and fathers, brothers and sisters, pray that we will all be faithful children of our Lord and reflections of the power and presence of Jesus Christ.

Proper 23
Pentecost 21
Ordinary Time 28
Luke 17:11-19
by Keith Hewitt

The Outsider

This was his favorite time of day. The sun was low, dipping behind the hills, and the sky was pearly gray, mottled with dark clouds, as though night had fled and left pieces of itself behind. He sat beneath a tree at the top of a hill and stared toward the horizon; letting the cool breeze wash away the worries of the day. Below, in the little pocket of a valley where the trail wound through, his companions were starting a fire and spreading blankets where they would sleep for the night.

Sure, there was always the chance of running into the occasional bandit, or bear, but he preferred sleeping out in the open, these nights, rather than in the smoky, stifling homes crammed together in the villages that marked the road between Galilee and Jerusalem. He let his head rest against the rough bark of the tree and breathed deeply of the cool, clean air.

Then a twig snapped and his eyes were suddenly open and alert, looking toward the sound. Almost instantly, they relaxed as they fell on the familiar form and face of the Teacher. He put one hand down next to himself, started to get up — stopped when the Teacher looked down at him and shook his head slightly. Instead, the Teacher sat down next to him and nodded toward the valley; he relaxed, and laid his head back again.

"So, Thomas — what happened today?" the Teacher asked, his voice gentle as his eyes.

Thomas turned his eyes toward the Teacher without moving his head, until he could see him out of the corners, looking almost sideways. He hesitated and then admitted frankly, "I don't know." Then he smiled, shrugged slightly. "But then, I often don't, until you've explained it to us."

"You're learning — you're all learning. But there is much to learn and little time."

Thomas frowned; he didn't like it when the Teacher spoke like that. As often as he was confused by what the man said, he was all too sure about what the Teacher meant when he talked about time being short... and it made him uncomfortable to know the *what* without understanding the *why* — if there was one.

"Do you understand leprosy?" the Teacher asked.

Thomas shrugged. "I don't know anyone who's had it, of course. But I know it's a sickness that attacks your body and makes you inhuman, unclean."

"It's more than just a painful, shameful sickness — it's more like a wall," the Teacher said, his face drawn down in a frown as he spoke. "It's a wall that's thrown up overnight, from the moment it's discovered, separating the leper from his family, from his home, and from his livelihood. When a man becomes a leper, he becomes unclean, and when he's unclean he's cut off from everything he ever held dear, from everything that *completed* him as a man. A man with leprosy is separated from who he could be, by what he's become."

Thomas nodded in the dim light. "It's a tragic illness."

"That's why the Samaritan was so full of praise when he returned. It was as though I had opened a gate through that wall by healing him — in any real sense of the word, I had given him his life back."

"I can see that," Thomas said slowly. "I think I understand. But then why did only the Samaritan return?"

It was the Teacher's turn to shrug. "Who can say?"

Thomas raised his head, then, and looked at him — smiled as he met his eyes. "Not I, Teacher — but I'm pretty sure *you* can."

The Teacher reflected his smile, nodded. "Perhaps it was because he was already an outsider, so he had a deeper appreciation of the pain of being apart from having a whole life. Or perhaps it was because he is not as closely tied to the priests of the Temple as the others and was willing to give thanks *outside* the walls of the Temple. Perhaps he recognized that he could give thanks to the Father through me and did not have to be in the Temple to do it."

Thomas studied the Teacher for a few moments — his expression was harder to see, now, in the gloom. "Teacher," he said slowly, "it is times like this that my head begins to hurt."

Another smile flickered in the shadows. "I'll leave you with this thought, then. Consider that sin is like leprosy — it disfigures men, makes them less than what they could be, and it cuts them off from the completeness of being in harmony with the Father. And now the Son of Man offers a chance to be cleansed, a chance to be healed — a way through the wall of sin, back into harmony with the Father, just as the leper who is cleansed of his disease can rejoin life."

The Teacher stood up, then, leaned down and stretched his hand to Thomas as he continued. "Like healing, forgiveness is there for anyone who has faith — perhaps it's right that an outsider should be the first to praise God for it. Perhaps it was easiest for *him* to recognize what it meant to have the chance to go home again."

He grasped Thomas' hand, pulled him up easily. They stood face-to-face for a moment, then, hands clasped — and it seemed to Thomas that the Teacher's grip held him tightly. "Know this, Thomas — I've come to take on their burdens and to share the gift of forgiveness with *all* men… but only those who are blessed with faith and truly understand their own nature, their own brokenness, will understand the power of forgiveness to make them whole, to bring them back to the Father again."

Thomas looked back at him steadily. "I think I understand."

The Teacher looked at him closely, nodded, and released his grip. "You begin to understand," he agreed, "but you have questions." Then he smiled. "With you, Thomas, there are always questions."

And so the two men continued to talk as they descended the hill, rejoining their companions in the valley.

Proper 24
Pentecost 22
Ordinary Time 29
Psalm 119:97-104
by C. David McKirachan

Deontologize the Principle of Parsimony

I had a hard time determining a major in college. I vacillated between History, Anthropology, English Lit., and Geology. I like field trips. There was one professor who fascinated me. He was older than the norm, played the cello, rode an ancient but shiny three-speed bike around the campus, enjoyed good sherry, chuckled around his pipe, and faced the tirades of adolescent arrogance with the aplomb of calm courage. His questions bothered me like fleas. I itched at them long after class. Dr. Strodach was a Philosophy professor. I took any class that had his name on it. I learned. He's why I majored in Philosophy. My father's Ph.D. from Princeton in Metaphysical Philosophy had absolutely nothing to do with it. Congenital disorders often go unnoticed.

Dr. Strodach gently goaded us toward a consideration of our own place in the world by inviting us to consider the monsters of the contemplative discipline. He refused to accept rote repetition of Plato. He wanted us to wrestle with the shadows on the wall of our own lives. What were our ideals? He poked holes in each and every balloon I lofted. And in the grand deflation, I discovered how the defense of my own foolishness limited my journey. He taught me not to tolerate fools. But he taught me how to have enough manners to not make myself one by considering myself far separated from their foolishness. This guy was the real deal. He reminded me of my father without all the Oedipal baggage.

In my senior year he got sick. Not the flu kind, the hospital surgery kind. We had just started a year-long trek through the metaphysicians. I was devastated. His replacement was a teacher who shall not be named here. The guy made me nuts. He loved to demonstrate his superior knowledge and use it like a lash to move us through the material. He was boring in lecture and did not deal well with questions no matter how insightful or desperate they were. The day we dealt with Occum's Razor was the final straw. This philosophic principle came from a Scottish monk, naturally. He said the simplest construction is best, the KISS principle comes from him. Keep it simple stupid. The not-so-esteemed professor held forth on the metaphysical chaos that swirls about our heads, calling forth Occum as the shining knight of logic to wield his razor in our defense. He then announced just what that razor was. "Deontologize the principle of parsimony." It was like getting a garbage compactor for a romantic gift (that's another story). It was like... This... boob (and that's generous) just cut himself with the razor he was showing us how to use. So much for keeping it simple.

In my stunned bewilderment, I suddenly heard Dr. Strodach chuckling. He never took his pipe out of his mouth. He just chuckled around it. I calmly held up my hand. Our ranting boob of a professor ground to a halt and glared at me. Raising his chin as to consider what kind of bug was presuming to disturb him, he pontificated, "Yes?" He made it a three-syllable word.

The bug humbly asked, "Sir, what does 'deontologize' mean?"

The boob stared at me, considering exactly what would be the best way to squash me. As realizing this gave him another moment to demonstrate his mental superiority, he launched into a tirade of multisyllabic balderdash. Finally considering me sufficiently squashed, he checked his notes and rebooted his destruction of Occum. I raised my hand again. He shuddered to another halt. He again addressed me with all the scorn of a Ph.D. to a fool. "Yes?" This time it was a four-syllable word.

The bug humbly begged, "Sir, what does 'parsimony' mean?"

Now to you this may not seem like a horribly offensive set of questions. You may have been wondering yourself. But to the class who had become numb under his lash it was clear there was a ray of Strodach sunshine beaming into our darkness. The boob stared at me for a good thirty seconds, looked at his notes, and dismissed the class.

Small victories mean a lot to slaves. We had to pass the class with a B if we were Philosophy majors. Small victory or not, we were still bugs in the amber of multisyllabic balderdash. I considered this as I plodded into the boob's room for the next class. I was waiting to pay for my small victory. I was late. The class was silent as I closed the door. I was afraid to turn around. As I came into the room, I saw Dr. Strodach sitting on the window sill smiling around his pipe. I was terrified that I would turn around and realize I was still in the boob's hell.

Dr. Strodach said to my back, "What's the matter Mr. McKirachan? I thought you believed in the resurrection of the body."

That good-humored master teacher gave me a gift, "sweeter than honey." He taught me the validity of grace under fire and demonstrated the courage to claim it. He also taught me that the truth will make us free.

God bless you, Dr. Strodach.

Proper 25
Pentecost 23
Ordinary Time 30
2 Timothy 4:6-8, 16-18
by Argile Smith

Looking Ahead

Jerry could hardly believe that he had been accepted! But, that's exactly what the dean of the university said in her letter to Jerry. Giddy with excitement, he held the letter in his hand and called Dawn, his wife of only a few months. She affirmed Jerry's dream of enrolling in graduate school. Now that he had been accepted, she favored the idea of uprooting themselves from North Carolina and moving to Los Angeles.

One other detail in the letter, however, caught Jerry and Dawn off guard. According to the dean, Jerry would be expected to enroll immediately for the next semester, which meant that he needed to relocate quickly. Jerry didn't really think that he would be accepted, so he hadn't done anything about getting ready to move.

Dawn insisted that he should go ahead to Los Angeles. She would stay in North Carolina and join him as soon as she could serve out her resignation notice at work, pack and load their belongings, and make the trek across the country. Reluctantly Jerry agreed and drove their "good" car to the place where his academic dream would come true, expecting Dawn to arrive shortly in a rented truck loaded with boxes and furniture.

For Jerry, the trip west went well. He made his way to the apartment complex where he and Dawn would make their new home without a problem. Getting from the new apartment to the university where he would study turned out to be easy too.

For Dawn, things didn't go so well. She had to go through the ordeal of packing up everything herself, and she had to handle her family's discomfort over her decision to drive across country alone. Of course, she also had to contend with her own fears about moving to a strange, new part of the world she had never visited before now.

Worst of all, she missed Jerry. Each day that passed since he left brought a new dimension to the pain she bore because she couldn't see him. As she came home from work every afternoon, her dread of nightfall became more difficult to bear. She and Jerry had always looked forward to that time of the day. At home after work, they had come to view nightfall as their time to be together, to revisit their dream for their future, to experiment with the new adventure of preparing dinner, and just to enjoy each other's company. That's why Dawn felt so sad when the sun set.

Of course, she and Jerry talked to each other all the time. Thanks to cell phones and the internet, they stayed in almost constant contact. They sent pictures to each other and corresponded on the moving details at every opportunity. Still, Dawn couldn't be with Jerry in person.

Finally, the day arrived for Dawn to hop in the truck and drive away from the home she had known for most of her life. Her parents noticed that she didn't seem to be sorrowful, but hopeful. When they asked her questions, she answered in ways that assured them of her eagerness to get on the road. When they brought up the new scenery, new opportunities, and new challenges of her new home, they asked her about what she looked forward to most of all once she reached her destination. Without batting an eye, she answered, "Seeing Jerry."

As Paul wrapped up his life, he told Timothy to look ahead. Living can be difficult, but Christians can look forward to seeing Jesus one day.

Reformation Day
Jeremiah 31:31-34
by Scott Dalgarno

A Change of Heart

Carol Lee and Jerry hadn't been married long. They had lots of love but little money. Living in the city they took what they could get: a one-bedroom, no-parking, apartment in a neighborhood where it was Halloween every day.

Sirens were ubiquitous and for every church there were six tattoo parlors. One of those was located right next door to their apartment house. Normally very accepting, Carol Lee was incensed by it. The place was busy until late every night. The people who showed up there were often loud, drunk, and even violent. Confrontations on the sidewalk in front of the place happened, it seemed, nightly. Carol Lee was livid. She'd walk all the way around the block to get to her apartment instead of taking a few steps to cross in front of the horrid shop.

"Come to bed," Jerry would insist, while Carol Lee would rip whoever she saw going in. This evening it looked like a single mother with two toddlers in tow. "That woman with the bleached blond hair obviously can't afford to feed her children and look, she's spending money on body art!"

When a man in their complex complained to the police about the noise, his Honda's tires were slashed. Things were getting bad. When Carol Lee brought up the parlor Jerry blew her off saying he wasn't getting involved and she better not either. His policy was simply, "Let's get the kind of jobs that'll pay us enough to get out of here." But Carol Lee couldn't think about that with little children suffering because of their mother's bad choices. She decided to do something that was entirely Carol Lee. She decided to get a tattoo.

Yep, she couldn't change them by hating them so she decided to get down and dirty with them. Maybe if she understood them better something would shift in her or maybe even in them. So, the question hung in the air: What kind of tattoo?

Carol Lee poured over books of quotations at the public library and settled on something by Madame de Stael. Armed with her choice, she showed up on the doorstep of the shop. She got there near noon when they opened. It was much too early for them to be busy. She'd found the walls of the place covered with pictures of naked women, knives and axes dripping blood, Nazi art, Our Lady of Guadalupe, the American flag in various positions, and human skulls.

Carl, the proprietor, was putting some Japanese lettering down a young woman's lovely neck. Carol Lee admitted to herself that it was tasteful if not beautiful.

Another artist, Enrique, asked if he could help her. "Yes," she said, "I want a tattoo. No art, just simple lettering to go around my left wrist."

"Saying what?"

She handed him the piece of torn notebook paper with the quote: "Who understands much, forgives much."

"Why this?" he asked.

Because I live next door and you guys scare me with your fighting and loud talk and scary customers," she said. "I want to understand you more so I can forgive you."

"Geez," said Enrique to Carl. "Dude, we got to stop fighting so much. We're scaring our neighbors."

Carl tried to downplay the problem but Carol Lee stopped him quickly, saying she wasn't there to complain. She just wanted to get a tattoo and get to know them a little bit while doing it.

That diffused everything. Carl smiled and Enrique laughed quietly and led Carol into the back where he opened a book of samples. He showed her a line from Hitler's Mein Kampf.

"No," said, Carol Lee, "I really want the quote about forgiveness."

Enrique really chuckled this time. "No," he said, "I'm not trying to get you to wear Nazi propaganda, but you still need to pick a writing design for me to copy."

Carol Lee laughed at her own ignorance. "Sure, sure, that's very nice. I'm sure it'd look less harsh in German."

In twenty minutes he was done and the words looked as delicate as her tiny wrist.

It seemed like overnight that Carl and Enrique became Carol Lee's best friends. She passed in front of their business many times every day now, waving and joking and showing everyone the lovely sentiment made even lovelier because she wore it with such pride.

The neighborhood changed too. No more fights broke out, and Enrique and Carl made sure the neighborhood was safe for all who lived there. Jerry and Carol would bring dinner down to the fellows and their families once a week or more. The bloody knives and swastikas disappeared from their walls and baskets of flowers now hung from the eaves of the business. People hardly recognized the place anymore. Police walked by now, shaking their heads.

All Saints Day
Daniel 7:1-3, 15-18
by Stan Purdum

Crazy Dreams

"Gee, Louise, you look pretty rough. And you're twenty minutes late, too." That was Alice's comment as her coworker finally got to her desk that Monday morning.

"I know," Louise said. "I didn't sleep very well again last night. And I decided to take the bus, and it was running a little behind."

"You rode the *bus*? How come? Your car in the shop?"

"No. I just thought it might be wise."

"You mean you're too sleepy to drive?"

"It's not that," Louise said, sighing. "You remember last week I told you I'd been having crazy dreams but couldn't remember what they were about when I woke up?"

"Sure."

"Well, for all three weekend nights, I've awakened remembering."

"This sounds *spooky*," Alice said with a shiver.

"Well, it sort of is. And it's why I had trouble going back to sleep."

"Tell me more."

"All my dreams are about cars. In one of Friday night's dreams, I was driving along a road to some place I wanted to go. I don't know where it was, but I was looking forward to getting there. But then I hit mud hole and got stuck. I couldn't get the car free."

"Well, that would be a problem, I guess, but it doesn't sound that scary."

"Except that the whole car started sinking into the mud hole, and I couldn't get out. The mud was just closing over the windows when I suddenly woke up."

"Oh. I see what you mean."

"Yes," said Louise, "but Saturday's dream was worse. I was driving a car in a race when the *steering wheel* came off in my hands. I couldn't get it back on and the car started careening all over the course. I woke up just before another car plowed into me."

"Ouch," said Alice.

"But last night's was worse yet. I was driving down a busy street with all three of my kids in the car, and suddenly, I drove over a cliff! I woke up as we were falling. I could even hear the kids screaming."

"Ah. So you took the bus because you are afraid all that stuff about cars was a warning about an accident or something next time you drove?"

"Yes. It makes sense, doesn't it?"

"I'm not so sure. Maybe you should talk to somebody who knows something about what dreams mean."

"You know somebody like that?"

"It happens that I do. He's a psych professor where my husband teaches. I bet he'd be willing to talk to you if you asked."

Louise considered Alice's suggestion and then said, "Maybe you're right. I don't want to keep putting in nights like these last ones. You have his number?"

A few days later, Louise and Alice were again talking in the office. Louise looked a lot better, and she had driven to work that morning.

"So what did Professor Benton say?" Alice asked.

"He said dreams are symbolic and that they usually aren't literally about the things in the dreams themselves. So he said that my dreams about the cars probably have nothing to do with automobiles or accidents but with something else altogether."

"Like what?"

"Like control. He said that if you dream of yourself in the driver's seat, you may mean that you see yourself as taking control of your life. But if, as in my dream, the car gets stuck in the mud, it may be symbolizing a feeling that I am are going nowhere, or that my life is in a rut."

"Does that fit you?"

"You bet."

"What about the crashes?"

"Yeah. That. Well, he said that dreaming that my car crashes could be my subconscious mind symbolizing that I feel my life is out of control."

"Wow. You look pretty calm for hearing all that."

"Well, I can't say it was good news," Louise said, "but it does fit how I've been feeling. And at least now I know I need to confront some stuff at home."

"So how'd you sleep last night?" Alice asked.

"Like a baby."

Proper 26
Pentecost 24
Ordinary Time 31
2 Thessalonians 1:1-4, 11-12
by Rick McCracken-Bennett

Small but Mighty Faithful

> ... *[W]e ourselves boast of you among the churches of God for your steadfastness and faith during all your persecutions and the afflictions that you are enduring.* — 2 Thessalonians 1:4

We all know of a congregation that is doing extraordinary work for the kingdom of God. Here is a story of one of them.

I often find myself speaking of a small church I once served. I had taken a ten-year hiatus from my work as a pastor and this was the church I served when I reentered.

I'll never forget the evening I met their Vestry and we hammered out an agreement that would amount to about a one third of my time spent in this small, rural, shrinking village. While the Vestry met to discuss whether or not to call me, I walked into the sanctuary and had a look around. My first thoughts bring me to shame upon remembering them. I stood in the pulpit and looked out at the smallest nave I had ever seen. Perhaps if you were careful you could squeeze a hundred in but sixty or seventy looked to be about the most it would hold. I remember thinking (I am ashamed to say) that I couldn't imagine preparing a sermon for only those few people. It was actually worse than that when I learned that only about forty folks showed up on any given Sunday.

But what was I to do? This would allow me to gradually get back into the active ministry while I kept my day job. It would work for now. It turns out that I stayed there joyfully for over eight years, the longest pastorate in the 100-year history of this church.

I, of course, quickly grew to love these people, their village, and the smell of the nave on Sunday before anyone else showed up. I preached, visited, married them, and buried them. It was a wonderful time in my life and the life of my family.

After I left, even though we had set up a cluster relationship to ease the financial burdens of this and two other churches, the congregation began to shrink from forty to less than 25 most times. And yet, they kept at it. Too proud to ask the diocese for money, they hunkered down and refused to give up. They looked the death of the congregation in the face and kept going with the mission and ministry of the church.

You see… this little church provided (at least) three essential ministries to that part of the county and no one in the congregation was willing to let those go.

Many years before, they had started a program that fed the elderly every weekday with a home-cooked meal, often with food from their own gardens, mixed with lots and lots of fun and fellowship. Though the program now received funding from outside the church, the congregational volunteers who work each and every day have kept this service available to the sixty or more people that showed up each day. I can't imagine that village without this program.

They also provided an "off-the grid" pantry. Though they understood why other pantries in the county could only allow a certain number of visits a month, this church decided to not link up with them and simply gave food to whoever came their way. That pantry continues solely on donations from the congregation and though they have no doubt been "taken" a time or two, they give gladly to the poor who come to their door week after week.

If that wasn't enough for a congregation of around 25 people, they provide a well-attended after-school tutoring program that, with the help of a small grant, allows them to have a certified teacher to lead their work.

Perhaps this doesn't sound like much. Certainly it pales in the sight of program- and corporate-sized churches and their work. But I wonder... what if every 25 people in our current congregations worked as faithfully in their mission and ministry? What would happen to the hunger, the illiteracy, and the loneliness in our parts of the mission field?

As you might imagine, I never tire of telling all I meet about this small but very faithful congregation. I never stop giving thanks to God for them.

Proper 27
Pentecost 25
Ordinary Time 32
Luke 20:27-38
by Frank Ramirez

The Wrong Lens

Four years and two years before he began kindergarten, our youngest son, Jacob, accompanied his older brother and sister to that special classroom. He was fascinated by the playground — especially the elephant slide. It was an ordinary enough slide but on the sides were painted elephants. Time and again he would ask if he could play on the elephant slide, but I always said no and that his time would come when it was his turn to go to school.

That made the approaching first day all the more exciting. As it grew nearer and nearer his excitement grew. Finally it came. He was dressed in a brand new outfit, with his equipment under his arm, but all of that was forgotten as he ran past the gate and into the play yard. Finally he would get a chance to play on the elephant slide. It was his turn.

As I parked he ran from the car into the playground, right up to the slide, and stopped short. I caught up. He had a stunned look on his face.

"What's wrong, Jacob?" I asked.

"Who shortened the slide?" he replied in alarm.

Nothing had changed. I took a look to make sure. Then it hit me. I was the same height then as I was the first day I brought his older brother to his first day. The slide looked the same to me.

But Jacob was four years older. And four years taller. The slide looked smaller to him!

I assured him that nothing had changed and the moment's suspicion gave way to a shrug and then a good ten minutes of fun on the slide before he was called in for the start of class.

* * *

The prophet Haggai did his best to inspire the people to rebuild the temple. The first temple had been destroyed by the Babylonians in 586 BC and many of the people had been taken away into exile. Now the Babylonians themselves had been conquered, and God's people had been sent home by the Persians, who encouraged their subject nations to retain their national identities, religions, and cultural practices — as long as they paid their taxes on time.

Sixteen years had passed since the return of the people, and there'd been problems with inertia, building permits, cooperation with the locals, and simply the great difficulties that went with getting resettled in a distant land. But finally building had begun.

Now those who had been children when the first temple was destroyed didn't think much of the second temple, and they said so, loudly. Haggai echoes their complaints when he asks, "Who is left among you that saw this house in its former glory? How does it look to you now? Is it not in your sight as nothing?" (Haggai 2:3).

But the reason it looked as nothing in their sight was they had seen the first temple as children — and it had looked huge. They had grown — not only in height, but in life experiences. They had endured two major disjunctures, the anguish that went with deportation and the joy of returning.

The present reality of the temple could not match their childhood memories. They were looking at the temple through the wrong lens, seeing the present reality but not perceiving it for what it was — and complaining loudly!

Haggai promised future prosperity and that "The latter splendor of this house shall be greater than the former..." (v. 9) but that promise could probably only come true when the naysayers and the complainers stepped aside. Just as Jacob had to accept the fact that the slide hadn't shrunk, but he had grown, so those in Haggai's day had to recognize they were quite as capable of matching the feat of building a magnificent temple, with God's help, as their ancestors. Indeed, though it took hundreds of years, the Great Temple of Jerusalem was, in Jesus' day, one of the great wonders of the world.

Looking through the wrong lens changes everything. When the Sadducees asked Jesus a question about a woman who married seven brothers, one after the other as she was widowed time and time again, they asked not as an academic exercise, nor as an honest debate about the meaning of scripture. They asked using the lens of skepticism — skepticism about the resurrection, skepticism about the scriptures, and especially skepticism about Jesus. They were incapable of recognizing that the Lord of Life, who would embody the resurrection, was in their midst.

We too must look at what God can accomplish in our midst but not through a lens that so glorifies the past that we discount the miracles of the present. It will do no good to adopt a pose of skepticism or despair. Trust and faith in God, and God's goodness will teach us that the present is good, despite what others tell us they see, and that the future will be glorious.

Proper 28
Pentecost 26
Ordinary Time 33
Luke 21:5-19; Isaiah 12
by Argile Smith

In That Day

Even though she had just turned her calendar to the month of October, the semester had already been too long for Kim. Her first semester at the university had been tough. The difficulties associated with adjusting to campus life, getting over syllabus shock, and learning how to sleep in a dorm paled in comparison to her almost constant ordeal with homesickness. At night, she would cry herself to sleep, thinking about her bed at home and her parents. She even missed her little brother, who had been nothing but a pest to her as far back as she could remember.

She could hardly wait for Thanksgiving break so she could return there for an entire week. That's why her heart sank to the floor when her mother called her to say that a trip for home at Thanksgiving wouldn't be possible. A strange and sudden change in plans at home left her with only one option: to drive up to her uncle's house for Thanksgiving Day. The rest of her time would be spent at school in the library or in front of her computer, and in either case, all by herself.

In her anger over what she considered to be unfair treatment, she emailed her mother about the change in plans and the devastation it had caused. First, Kim blamed her for being insensitive and thoughtless. She went on to remind her mother of the favored treatment her little brother had received all of his life, adding that he had been away at school, such a change in plans wouldn't have been considered at all!

Kim sent her searing message and sat there in her dorm room. The late afternoon sun cast a sad glow over her sullen face while tears of disappointment trickled down her cheek. She waited for a minute and wondered if she had done the right thing. After all, her mom couldn't do anything about the change of plans. Kim's dad wanted to visit his mother who had been sick for a long time. In fact, the doctors agreed that the past couple of birthdays had not been good to her frail frame and that no medicine could be prescribed that would stretch out her days. Kim's dad didn't want to live in regret over not making one last visit, and Kim's mom understood completely. That's why she made arrangements for Kim to spend Thanksgiving with her brother and his wife, Kim's favorite relatives.

But at the moment Kim didn't think about her dad's need to see his mother. She could only think about her agony over needing to see her folks and the home she missed so much.

Two hours passed before Kim got a reply from her mom. She wrote, "Sweet Kim, I knew that not being home at Thanksgiving would break your heart. I understand why you are mad at me. Keep in mind that Thanksgiving is just a few weeks away from the end of the semester. On that day, you can put your papers and exams behind you and come for a long Christmas break. It will make having to wait worthwhile. Keep thinking about that day, and it will help you to get through the days between now and then. And remember that no matter how you feel about me, I love you."

In time, Kim took her mother's advice to heart. She began to see every setting sun as a signal that she would have one less day to wait until she could go home.

Christ the King
Proper 29
Jeremiah 23:1-6
by C. David McKirachan

What's the Stick For?

When I started this job, over thirty years ago, I was amazed at people's intransigence. They didn't want to change, even when it made sense. I knew the new ideas made sense, because they made sense to me. God, I was young. "We never did it that way before" was their perfectly logical reason to keep doing things that were not only irrelevant and unnecessary but sometimes patently self-destructive. I used to grind my teeth and pound the pavement, trying to walk off the frustration.

I remember the first time someone set me up for the express purpose of hurting me and destroying the good the church was trying to do. It was like finding a pit dug in an interstate for no reason except to hurt and disrupt. It was a bloodless form of terrorism, right in my own backyard. It wounded my sense of hope. Working creatively for the kingdom had never been defensive for me. How could I trust? Some of the flock were carrying bombs.

It made me reconsider my attitude toward evil. It made me realize that part of my call was not only to take advantage of the church as a staging area for rescuing the lost but to also make sure that this sanctuary was really safe. Evil wasn't only out there. I remembered the Lord's words, "The Kingdom of God is *among*, or it could be *within* us." I had just discovered that the "dark side" was also *among* or it could be *within* us.

I had always been taught to be humble, non-judgmental, and, in a word, nice. I began considering the nature of the abuse that flourishes in a home where people try their best to be loving and end up enabling. Yes, the abusers are themselves victims, but being merely nice to them will not help them or their victims. People who were bent on exercising their muscles of domination and control in the church were suffering under burdens of anger and hurt. The best way I could minister to them was to confront their behavior and protect the family of faith.

I worked at Johnsonburg Camp as a volunteer. It's 400-odd acres of woods in northwestern New Jersey. On one hike I found a red cedar branch, heavy at one end, knotted and gnarled as cedar can be. I'd taken it and worked with it, hand and pocket knife, until it became a smooth staff, too heavy for a walking stick. I put it in the corner of my office at the church. It reminded me of my responsibility as a pastor. We're here to care for the flock. We keep them together. We scope out new pastures and good water. We help them lamb and keep them healthy and out of holes. We also keep the predators away. Wolves aren't sheep. That's one reason shepherds carry a big stick.

But the staff is also there to remind me that the evil I have to watch for is not only out there somewhere — it is also within. It is as close as a budget meeting or a ladies' circle. It is as close as my own arrogance and self-righteousness. Woe to us if we forget. We'll be on the menu.

Thanksgiving Day
John 6:25-35
by Keith Hewitt

Bread

She was sitting at the kitchen table when her son returned with a jarring door slam and a triumphant, "I'm back!"

She leaned to her right so she could peek out toward the living room where he was busily shedding his Evil Jester costume. A navy blue pillow case sat on the floor next to him, bulging with treats. "Did you have fun?"

"Yeah! We went farther tonight than last year — all the way down to the tracks and back. Katy's dad jumped out of the bushes down on Harding in a Grim Reaper costume and chased us for two blocks." He dropped his mask, held up the bag and shook it; the rustle of candy wrappers was loud. "I'll be eating candy 'til Christmas!"

"Oh... good," she said unenthusiastically and straightened in her chair to get back to dealing with the business at hand. "Don't forget to check everything before you eat it," she called out absently, mind already focusing on the bills and checkbook in front of her. Was it her imagination or was the stack of bills actually higher this month? She shook her head; it was time to bite the bullet and dig in. She reached for the first unopened bill, slit the envelope, and pulled out the contents.

Suddenly: "Be right back! I forgot something!" And with that, he was gone, out the door before she could ask what he'd forgotten, or where he was going.

"Boys," she murmured, and glanced at the clock — not quite 7:00 yet, even though it was already dark. Still early enough. She turned her attention back to the bill, wrote down the balance and minimum payment, slipped it back into the envelope and set it aside. There was time to do this to a dozen or so bills before the front door slammed again. "Where were you?" she called, before he could even announce his return.

"I forgot Mrs. Bailey's," he explained, walking toward the kitchen. His footsteps were soft, cushioned by the soles of his costume.

"Mrs. Bailey?"

"The church lady." He was in the doorway to the kitchen, now, with a small, clear plastic bag. In it, a round loaf of bread about the size of two hands side by side was still warm enough to cause condensation on the inside of the bag. "You know, she makes the communion bread, and the kids get whatever's left over in Sunday school."

"Right — Mrs. Bailey."

"If she knows you, you get bread for a treat — and I almost forgot!" He peeled apart the seal at the top of the bag, reached in, and pulled the bread out. The scent of fresh-baked bread filled the kitchen almost immediately. It was a magical smell — at once it reminded her of church and communion — but also of home, and childhood, and her mother's fresh bread.

She took a deep breath, held the memories close, and then exhaled reluctantly. "I understand why you wanted to go back out."

"Who wouldn't? This is the best stuff in the world." He tore off a piece, offered it to his mother. "Want some?" She hesitated but a moment, then took it and bit off a smaller piece, let it sit on her tongue for a bit before she finally chewed slowly, letting the taste roll over her as the bread almost melted in her mouth. When that sensation started to fade, she took another bite, let it flow through her senses — smell, taste, texture…

If she could have heard it, it would have sounded like a choir of angels.

Her son took his own piece and then set the loaf aside. "You know," he said, "Halloween is my favorite holiday, and I really like trick-or-treating — but all of *that* stuff —" he tilted his head back toward the living room, where the sack of candy sat on the floor, "— I can't live on that. Sure, it tastes good when you first eat it, and it's sweet and all, but it doesn't fill you up, and after a while it just doesn't taste good."

He tore off another piece of bread, ate it slowly, speaking around it. "But this stuff, I could live on. I know we get the same bread at church every month, and it's the same bread she hands out for Halloween — but every time I eat it, it's like there's a different combination of flavors and how it feels. Sometimes it's crustier, sometimes it's saltier, or sweeter — but it's still the same. Do you know what I mean?"

"I think so," his mother said. "No matter how often you eat it, it's a little like the first time — but still familiar."

"Right. And it's *always* good." He offered another piece to her. "I know candy is good, but it's not good for me, and it's not real food. But this will always fill me up."

His mother took the piece and nodded. "That it will," she agreed. Then, gently, "Now why don't you get out of that costume? Your father will be home soon, and then we'll have dinner."

He smiled. "I may not be hungry by then."

After he left — with the bread — she sighed once more and turned back to the bills and budget... but suddenly it didn't seem quite as important. With the taste and smell of bread still lingering, and a warm fullness in her belly, it was hard to worry. Yes, the worries of life would be back soon enough.

But then there was always the bread...

About the Authors

David O. Bales was a Presbyterian (USA) pastor for 33 years, and is a graduate of the University of Portland (where he was editor of the yearbook) and San Francisco Theological Seminary. In addition to his ministry, he also has taught college: World Religions, Ethics, Biblical Hebrew and Biblical Greek (recently at College of Idaho). He has been a freelance researcher, writer, and editor for Stephen Ministries. His sermons and articles have appeared in *Interpretation, Pulpit Digest, Preaching, Lectionary Homiletics, Emphasis,* and *Preaching the Great Texts*. He wrote a year-long online column: "In The Original: Insights from Greek and Hebrew for the Lectionary Passages." His books include: *Gospel Subplots: Story Sermons of God's Grace; Toward Easter and Beyond; Scenes of Glory: Subplots of God's Long Story;* and *To the Cross and Beyond: Cycle A Sermons for Lent and Easter,* all available at CSS Publishing Company.

Scott Dalgarno is pastor of Wasatch Presbyterian Church in Salt Lake City, Utah. Born in California, he has previously served four Presbyterian churches in Oregon. He is a graduate of Whitworth University, University of Oregon, and San Francisco Theological Seminary. A poet, his poems have appeared in *The Christian Century, America, The Antioch Review,* and *Yale Review*.

Sandra Herrmann is a retired pastor and popular teacher in the Wisconsin Conference of the United Methodist Church. She is a poet and the author of *Ambassadors of Hope* (CSS). She has been published in *alive now!*, a magazine of spirituality of the UMC, *Emphasis* magazine for pastors, and currently writes monthly for *StoryShare*. She is working on a book exploring the Christian iconography of the Harry Potter series.

Keith Hewitt is the author of two volumes of *NaTiVity Dramas: Nontraditional Christmas Plays for All Ages* (CSS). He is a local pastor, co-youth leader, an occasional speaker at Christmas events, and former Sunday school teacher at Wilmot United Methodist Church in Wilmot, Wisconsin. He lives in southeastern Wisconsin with his wife, two children, and assorted dogs and cats.

Craig Kelly received his B.A. from the University of Saskatchewan in 2002. He and his wife, Beth, are actively involved in their church, working both in their church's children's ministry as well as working with low-income youth in their neighborhood. Craig enjoys reading, music, hiking, biking, and indulging in old sci-fi movies.

C. David McKirachan is pastor of the Presbyterian Church at Shrewsbury in central New Jersey. He also teaches at Monmouth University. McKirachan is the author of *I Happened Upon a Miracle* and *A Year of Wonder* (Westminster John Knox).

Rick McCracken-Bennett is an Episcopal priest, storyteller, writer, musician, and church planter. He is a member of the Storytellers of Central Ohio and the National Storytelling Network. His doctoral dissertation concerned the use of story to guide congregations into the future that God intends for them. He is the rector of All Saints Episcopal Church in New Albany, Ohio, where a sermon wouldn't be a sermon without a good story.

Stan Purdum, a United Methodist minister, is a freelance writer and editor. His books include *He Walked in Galilee*, about the ministry of Jesus (Abingdon Press, 2005) and *New Mercies I See*, short stories about God's grace (CSS Publishing Company, Inc., 2003), as well as four books about bicycling. He has been published in religious and secular journals, has authored numerous sermons for lectionary volumes and preaching journals, and writes adult Sunday school curriculum. Stan and his wife, Jeanine, live in North Canton, Ohio. They have three grown children.

Frank Ramirez has served as a pastor for nearly 30 years in Church of the Brethren congregations in Los Angeles, California; Elkhart, Indiana; and Everett, Pennsylvania. A graduate of LaVerne College and Bethany Theological Seminary, Ramirez is the author of numerous books, articles, and short stories. His CSS titles include *Partners in Healing*, *He Took a Towel*, *The Bee Attitudes*, and three volumes of *Lectionary Worship Aids*.

Argile Smith is Vice President for Advancement at William Carey University in Hattiesburg, Mississippi. He previously served at New Orleans Baptist Theological Seminary (NOBTS) as a preaching professor, chairman of the Division of Pastoral Ministries, and director of the communications center. While at NOTBS, Smith regularly hosted the Gateway to Truth program on the FamilyNet television network. He has also been the pastor of several congregations in Louisiana and Mississippi. Smith's articles have been widely published in church periodicals, and he is the author or editor of four books.

Peter Andrew Smith is an ordained minister in the United Church of Canada, currently serving St. James United Church in Antigonish, Nova Scotia. He is the author of *All Things Are Ready* (CSS), a book of lectionary-based communion prayers. He is also the author of a number of stories and articles, which can be found listed at www.peterandrewsmith.com.

The Rt. Rev. John S. Smylie, Bishop of Wyoming, previously served as the rector of St. Mark's Episcopal Church in Casper, Wyoming, and as the dean of the Cathedral of St. John the Evangelist in Spokane, Washington. He is a published author and storyteller as well as a singer-songwriter. Smylie recently completed *Grace for Today*, a collection of 25 stories that explores how grace, loss, and restoration are part of the same fabric.

John Sumwalt is the pastor of Our Lord's United Methodist Church in New Berlin, Wisconsin, and a noted storyteller. He is the author of nine books, including the acclaimed *Vision Stories* series and *How to Preach the Miracles: Why People Don't Believe Them and What You Can Do About It*. John and his wife Jo Perry-Sumwalt served for three years as the co-editors of *StoryShare*. A graduate of the University of Wisconsin-Madison and the University of Dubuque Theological Seminary (UDTS), Sumwalt received the Herbert Manning Jr. award for parish ministry from UDTS in 1997.

www.ingramcontent.com/pod-product-compliance
Lightning Source LLC
Chambersburg PA
CBHW071718040426
42446CB00011B/2116